Arnold P. Goldstein, Ph.D., a professor of psychology at Syracuse University, is noted for his studies in behavioral psychology and is a prolific author who has written or edited eighteen books.

Robert P. Sprafkin, Ph.D., an associate adjunct professor of psychology at Syracuse University, is the director of the Day Treatment Center at Syracuse Veterans Administration Hospital.

N. Jane Gershaw, Ph.D., an adjunct assistant professor of psychology at Syracuse University and clinical assistant professor of Psychiatry at the State University of New York, Upstate Medical Center, is also a practicing psychotherapist who, along with Drs. Goldstein and Sprafkin, wrote *Skill Training for Community Living.*

I Know What's Wrong,
But I Don't Know What to Do About It

Arnold P. Goldstein
Robert P. Sprafkin
N. Jane Gershaw

A SPECTRUM BOOK

Prentice-Hall, Inc., Englewood Cliffs, New Jersey 07632

Libary of Congress Cataloging in Publication Data

Goldstein, Arnold P
  I know what's wrong, but I don't know what to do about
it.

  (The Transformation Series) (A Spectrum Book)
  Bibliography: p.
  Includes index.
  1.   Success.   2. Behavior modification.   I.   Sprafkin,
Robert P., joint author.   II. Gershaw, N. Jane, joint
author.   III.   Title
BF637.S8G64   158'.1   78-24015
ISBN 0-13-448795-8
ISBN 0-13-448787-7 pbk.

A Spectrum Book

10 9 8 7 6 5 4 3 2 1

Printed in the United States of America

Editorial–production supervision
and interior design by Eric Newman
Cover design by Hernandez Porto
Manufacturing buyer: Cathie Lenard

PRENTICE-HALL INTERNATIONAL, INC., *London*
PRENTICE-HALL OF AUSTRALIA PTY. LIMITED, *Sydney*
PRENTICE-HALL OF CANADA, LTD., *Toronto*
PRENTICE-HALL OF INDIA PRIVATE LIMITED, *New Delhi*
PRENTICE-HALL OF JAPAN, INC., *Tokyo*
PRENTICE-HALL OF SOUTHEAST ASIA, PTE. LTD., *Singapore*
WHITEHALL BOOKS LIMITED, *Wellington, New Zealand*

To our families

Contents

ix, *Preface*

1

1, *How to Use This Book*

2

9, *Knowing What's Wrong:*
Diagnosing the Problem

3

31, *Getting Ready:*
Preparing to Change Your Behavior

4

43, *What to Do About It:
Changing Your Behavior*

5

55, *Personal Skills in Action:
Guidelines, Steps, and Examples*

6

111, *Making Changes Stick*

7

121, *More Personal Skills*

131, *Bibliography:
Structured Learning Therapy Research*

135, *Index*

Preface

Negotiating . . . preparing for a stressful conversation . . . giving a compliment . . . responding to failure . . . expressing affection . . . making decisions . . . controlling your anger . . . asserting yourself. These are some of the 48 skills described in this book, along with a practical, step-by-step method called Structured Learning by which you can learn them. The skills are those we all need to lead satisfying and effective lives at home, at work, in our social lives, and elsewhere. They are also skills that may help you to feel more self-confident in a variety of situations you currently avoid or find uncomfortable.

We are three behavioral psychologists who have worked for many years helping people *act* differently with others and *feel* better about themselves. We have trained hundreds of people, from all walks of life, to be consistently effective in using the interpersonal and personal skills taught in this book to lead fuller, more satisfying lives in today's complex world. We are not advice-givers but are more like teachers who can help you to learn skills that you may have never learned, or sharpen and refine skills that you may find difficult. We will teach you how to diagnose your skill strengths and skill weaknesses and then, after you know what's wrong, we'll teach you what to do about it.

ACKNOWLEDGMENTS

A number of people have made contributions to this book in important ways, contributions we most sincerely appreciate. Much of our thinking originally grew from our interaction with the members of our Syracuse University Interpersonal Skills Workshop. We owe a real debt to the fertile ideas of these Workshop students. Several of our graduate students have also helped us a great deal. Dana O'Brien, Eric Edelman, Debbie Strum, and David Bleeker were especially resourceful in their efforts to build and refine the book's Skill Questionnaire. Don MacGregor, Evelyn Taylor, Shirley Sommers, and Sally Segal were chief among the many consultants who provided us with useful feedback regarding our training procedures. Early drafts of this book were read by Bonnie Wolf. Her reactions and suggestions were candid and thoughtful, and they helped us see our writing in new perspectives. Eric Newman, our friend and editor at Prentice-Hall, who contributed significantly to both this book's editing and production, clearly deserves our special thanks.

I Know What's Wrong . . .

1

How to Use This Book

Ellen Harris* has three children, two of them teenagers. Ellen and her children got along reasonably well when they were younger, but in recent years, their relationship has gotten worse and worse. They don't talk to one another very often, and when they do they usually end up arguing. There are misunderstandings, poor communication, distance, and hostility, very little of which used to be part of their lives. Ellen has really come to know what "generation gap" means. She finds it harder and harder to feel good about herself as a parent. Today she told her daughter to straighten up her room before going out. Five minutes later they were shouting at each other, Ellen in tears, her daughter on her way out of the house in a rage. Among other things, Ellen has to become more effective in the skills *expressing a complaint, persuading others,* and *giving instructions.*

Al and Barbara Benson are also having problems, with each other. Sex, money, and the kids are what their problems seem to be about . . . at first glance. If one looks deeper, however, one will see that they each seem to be unable or unwilling to understand and respond to each other's feelings.

*The names used in this book are fictitious. However, the situations described are representative of the problems of many people with whom we have come into contact.

As they've grown apart, their empathy for each other and their ability to *express affection* to each other has grown less and less. Moreover, their ability to *express anger* constructively has all but disappeared.

Paul Johnson works in a large Eastern manufacturing company. He's married, a father of two, and is, more often than not, a rather unhappy person. Paul tends to be quite timid and unassertive. He rarely volunteers his ideas at work, although he has many good ones. He rarely tells his wife what he would like to do socially, although there are certain activities that he prefers. He has never asked his boss for a raise; he simply takes whatever has come along. He can't recall ever having talked back to a pushy salesperson or to someone who stepped in front of him in line. In many ways, Paul would be a happier and more competent person if he could somehow just learn to *be more assertive* and better able to *respond to persuasion* from others.

Harry Thomas, at age 24, has almost the opposite problem. At work and at home, Harry has great difficulty controlling his temper with friends. The little inconveniences and minor frustrations that most people ignore often set Harry off. Just this month he's had two loud arguments at work, made a noisy scene in a restaurant when the waiter seemed too slow, ended a date very early in a "fit of temper," and almost come to blows with a shirt salesman in a department store. Harry needs to learn such skills as *using self control, responding to a complaint*, and *negotiating*.

Finally, let's look at Tom Allison. For the past three months, Tom has been managing a middle-sized service organization. But he's not making it as a manager. Product quality is down and absenteeism is up. Certain work methods changes will go into effect in a few weeks and he's afraid his people won't accept them. Tom is weak on just those leadership and planning skills vital for successful managers: *setting a goal, gathering information, setting problem priorities,* and *making a decision.*

We have just described a small number of people in difficulty. What they share in common are deficiencies in a variety of skills that are important in being effective, feeling personally satisfied, and in getting along well with others. They also share in common the price in unhappiness and unfulfilled aspirations that they pay for these personal and interpersonal skill deficiencies. Some people with these problems seek professional help from a psychotherapist or counselor. Much more often, however, they will turn first to a friend, loved one, or other "interested helper." The helper will pay attention, express concern and, most typically, offer advice—usually of the "don't worry," "hang in there," "wait it out," "try harder" variety. Unfortunately, though their intentions are good, their advice has very limited value. It usually provides welcome support, but people who lack specific abilities or skills necessary to live happily and effectively often need more than just support and friendship. At best, such help works temporarily. For some, professional help from a psychotherapist or counselor is a wise alternative. But for many people lacking or deficient in one or more interpersonal, social, aggression control or planning skills, there is another option to consider, an alternative we will describe in detail throughout this book. We'll make clear how people like Ellen Harris can learn to express a complaint or give instructions to members of her family, how couples like the Bensons can learn to share empathy and affection with each other, how unassertive individuals like Paul Johnson can develop the skill of speaking up for themselves in a firm and direct manner, how short tempers and explosive anger can be exchanged for self-control, and how planning skills, such as those central to Tom Allison's career, can be learned and used in effective and satisfying ways. These are examples of the goals to which this skill-training book is dedicated. We want to help you identify, learn, and apply the skills you need for a more enjoyable and effective daily life.

First, we'll help you identify both the skills you're already competent in and the ones you need to improve upon. Chapter 2 is specifically designed to help you identify these skill strengths and weaknesses. It consists of the Skill Questionnaire, a self-administered test that will provide you with information about your interpersonal behavior. Once you've taken stock of you skills in this manner, you'll be ready to prepare to improve your skillfullness. Chapter 3 describes a set of techniques that will help you do this. Using these techniques will greatly increase your chances of learning your chosen skills rapidly and thoroughly. These preparation techniques are: (1) setting specific behavior-change goals for yourself, (2) establishing "contracts" to increase the chances you'll reach these goals, and (3) getting help or support from others so that they will also help you meet your skill-improvement objectives. Chapter 3, therefore, is a step-by-step discussion of the procedures that should be used to accomplish these three preparation purposes of setting goals, establishing contracts, and getting support.

Once you've prepared, you're ready to work on the skills themselves. Chapter 4 describes a proven method for learning new skill behaviors most rapidly and effectively. In that chapter we present in detail the specific procedures that make up this method, called Structured Learning. We first saw the value of Structured Learning in our clinical work as psychologists. We and others followed up this clinical work with a research program that provided us with experimental evidence that Structured Learning was indeed effective. (This research is described in the books and articles listed in the bibliography.) For this reason, we feel strongly that the

Structured Learning method can lead you to rapidly increase your level of skill effectiveness.

Once you've learned how the method works, you'll be ready to learn more about the skills you've chosen to work on. In Chapter 5, *Personal Skills in Action,* you'll find detailed information about the skills tested in your Skill Questionnaire—what each skill is, the specific behavioral steps that make it up, examples of how to use it properly, and examples of how you might use it improperly. Armed with the skills' behavioral steps and good examples of their use, you can start to use the preparation and Structured Learning procedures you've read about in order to learn your target skills.

It's often true, unfortunately, that people may learn new skills, but their learning may not transfer to the situations in which they really need to use the skills. To maximize the chances that your new skills will be there where and when you need them, and to minimize the possibility of their loss, the next part of the book (Chapter 6) describes several procedures that will help turn your new skills into lasting habits. Finally, there are several skills that, while perhaps less troublesome for many people than the skills described in Chapter 5, can still often be a problem. These skills, and their behavioral steps, are listed in Chapter 7.

CHAPTERS AND THEIR PURPOSES

1. *How to Use This Book*
   Purpose: Orientation and overview
2. *Knowing What's Wrong: Diagnosing the Problem*
   Purpose: Identify your skill strengths and weaknesses.

3. *Getting Ready: Preparing to Change Your Behavior*
   Purpose: Set specific skill improvement goals, contract with yourself to increase your motivation to reach your goals, enlist the help of others.

4. *What to Do About It: Changing Your Behavior*
   Purpose: Describe the Structured Learning method and how to use its four procedures: behavioral descriptions, behavioral rehearsal, behavioral feedback, and behavioral transfer.

5. *Personal Skills in Action: Guidelines, Steps, and Examples*
   Purpose: Describe and define the complete series of difficult skills, present the behavioral steps that make up each skill, give examples of good and poor skill use.

6. *Making Changes Stick*
   Purpose: Describe several procedures for making your skill improvement last.

7. *More Personal Skills*
   Purpose: Describe and define additional skills. Present the behavioral steps that make up each skill.

We wish you success in applying the methods and materials in this book to your own skill learning and hope that its use will lead you to a more skilled, more satisfying, and more effective life.

2

Knowing What's Wrong: Diagnosing the Problem

The first step in solving any problem involves diagnosing, or defining what it is. This may sound like an easy thing to do, but actually, most people have a hard time looking at problem situations. For example, someone who feels tense or fearful at a party may not understand exactly what's contributing to that discomfort. Or someone who's afraid to accept a date may not recognize precisely which aspects of dating are frightening.

Talking about problems in general terms, such as "disliking parties," "being shy," or "having trouble dating," is helpful only in identifying broad problem areas. What we will help you to do in this chapter is pinpoint your difficulties in a way that makes them specific, and therefore more manageable and easier to resolve. Think about it. How might you go about solving the problem of "disliking parties"? You can't possibly deal constructively with something as broad, vague, and complex as "disliking parties." But you can identify a number of specific aspects of the broader problem area. The key to doing this is taking a close look at your own behavior in difficult situations. What skills do you use in those situations and how well do you use them?

Let's look at an example. Mary Ann complains that one of the reasons she doesn't like parties is that no one talks to her. In looking at her own behavior in most party situations, she realizes that, actually, she doesn't do very much to encourage others to talk to her. She enters the room, finds an out-of-the-way chair, and says to herself, "I wish someone would notice me." What skills might she use to turn the situation around? Perhaps she could try "Starting a Conversation" or "Listening" (see pages 59 and 63). Once she has done these, and has therefore made a beginning effort to involve herself at the party, she might try the skills "Expressing a Compliment" or "Responding to the Feelings of Others" (see pages 65 and 80).

How can you identify the skills you want to work on in situations where you are "uncomfortable," "uneasy," or "ineffective"? One good way is to think about the overall problem and then try to break it down, as Mary Ann did. Look at the skills on the following list. Would any of them help you cope better with the situation? Can you find any skills that you use particularly well or any in which you need work?

SKILL LIST

1. Starting a conversation
2. Ending a conversation
3. Listening
4. Expressing a compliment
5. Asking for help
6. Giving instructions
7. Expressing affection
8. Expressing a complaint
9. Persuading others
10. Expressing anger

11. Responding to a compliment
12. Responding to the feelings of others
13. Following instructions
14. Responding to persuasion
15. Responding to failure
16. Responding to contradictory messages
17. Responding to a complaint
18. Concentrating on a task
19. Preparing for a stressful conversation
20. Making a decision
21. Determining responsibility
22. Using self-control
23. Negotiating
24. Being assertive

You should now go on to the Skill Questionnaire, which follows. It will help you to further identify your skill strengths and weaknesses. Read each item carefully and answer each one as honestly as you can by putting a check mark in the column that best describes *your* typical use of the skill. Once you've finished your Skill Questionnaire, you'll be ready to select the specific skills you want to work on.

SKILL QUESTIONNAIRE

| | Always or Almost Always | Sometimes | Hardly Ever or Never |

1. *Starting a Conversation:* Talking to someone about light topics and then leading into more serious topics.
   (a) When I enter a room of people, I am comfortable introducing myself to someone and beginning a conversation. ___ ___ ___
   (b) I feel comfortable beginning a conversation with my boss or teacher. ___ ___ ___
   (c) In a store, I start conversations with salespeople when I want to know more about a product. ___ ___ ___

2. *Ending a Conversation:* Letting another person know that you've been paying attention, and then skillfully closing the conversation.
   (a) When I'm at a social gathering, I end conversations without feeling awkward. ___ ___ ___
   (b) When my boss or teacher starts a conversation with me, I feel comfortable ending it when necessary. ___ ___ ___
   (c) When I want to end a telephone conversation with a friend or relative, I do it easily. ___ ___ ___

SKILL QUESTIONNAIRE *(cont.)*

	1	2	3
	Always or Almost Always	Sometimes	Hardly Ever or Never

3. *Listening:* Paying attention to someone who is talking and making an effort to understand what's being said.
   - (a) I'm able to listen when my spouse wants to tell me about his or her day. ___ ___ ___
   - (b) When my child comes to me with a problem, I listen carefully. ___ ___ ___
   - (c) I listen carefully when my boss or teacher is telling me what to do. ___ ___ ___

4. *Expressing a Compliment:* Telling others that you like something about them or about their actions.
   - (a) I tell my teacher I enjoyed his or her lecture. ___ ___ ___
   - (b) I make an effort to compliment friends for things they've done. ___ ___ ___
   - (c) I praise my children when they've done well in school. ___ ___ ___

5. *Asking for Help:* Requesting that someone help you in handling a difficult situation.
   - (a) I'm comfortable asking my spouse to help me with a difficult chore. ___ ___ ___

SKILL QUESTIONNAIRE *(cont.)*

	1	2	3
	Always or Almost Always	Sometimes	Hardly Ever or Never

    (b) I'm comfortable asking my friend to help me solve a personal problem. — — —

    (c) I ask co-workers for help in my job. — — —

6. *Giving Instructions:* Clearly explaining to someone how you would like a specific task done.

    (a) I tell friends what to bring to a party I'm giving. — — —

    (b) I give instructions to my spouse on what to buy at the store. — — —

    (c) I give instructions to a repairman at my home or office. — — —

7. *Expressing Affection:* Letting others know that you care about them.

    (a) I'm comfortable telling my friends how much I care for them. — — —

    (b) I comfortably tell my spouse I love him or her. — — —

    (c) I express my affection to my family members (parents, children, brothers, sisters). — — —

8. *Expressing a Complaint:* Telling others that they are responsible for creating particular

	1	2	3
	Always or Almost Always	Sometimes	Hardly Ever or Never

problems for you and attempting to find solutions for the problems.

(a) I easily express a complaint to my friends that are in the habit of arriving late to appointments. ___ ___ ___

(b) When my boss gives me too much work to do, I express my complaint. ___ ___ ___

(c) I express a complaint to a waitress about a meal that isn't cooked well. ___ ___ ___

9. *Persuading Others:* Attempting to convince others that your ideas are better and will be more useful than theirs.

(a) I persuade my spouse to watch the TV program I have been waiting to see. ___ ___ ___

(b) I persuade my friend to go to a party with me. ___ ___ ___

(c) I persuade my classmate or co-worker to support my point of view on an issue that affects both of us. ___ ___ ___

10. *Expressing Anger:* Communicating your angry feelings to someone in a direct and honest manner.

(a) I express my angry feelings to my

	1	2	3
	Always or Almost Always	Sometimes	Hardly Ever or Never

spouse for accepting a party invitation when he or she knew I wanted to stay home. ___ ___ ___

(b) I express my angry feelings to my friends for not telling me about their change in plans. ___ ___ ___

(c) I express my angry feelings to a co-worker for leaving the hardest part of the job for me. ___ ___ ___

11. *Responding to a Compliment:* Letting others know that you're pleased by their compliments and that you appreciate them.

(a) I accept a compliment from my friend about my appearance without feeling awkward. ___ ___ ___

(b) I accept a compliment from my spouse when I've done something thoughtful. ___ ___ ___

(c) I feel comfortable when I'm at a meeting and am praised for doing good work. ___ ___ ___

12. *Responding to the Feelings of Others:* Trying to understand what another person is feeling.

(a) I understand how my spouse feels when

	1	2	3
	Always or Almost Always	Sometimes	Hardly Ever or Never

he or she arrives home after a difficult day.

   (b) I can tell what or how my friends are feeling when they call me up and "just want to talk."

   (c) I can tell what my co-workers are feeling even if they don't say a word.

13. *Following Instructions:* Paying attention to instructions, giving your reactions, and carrying them out adequately.

   (a) When I go shopping for my spouse, I buy the things that he or she asked me to get.

   (b) I follow instructions carefully when my co-worker explains a new office procedure to me.

   (c) I follow the instructions given to me to get someplace I've never been before.

14. *Responding to Persuasion:* Carefully and seriously considering another person's position, weighing it against your own, and then deciding which will be best for you in the long run.

	1	2	3
	Always or Almost Always	Sometimes	Hardly Ever or Never

(a) When a co-worker tries to persuade me to contribute for a gift for someone I don't know well, I resist that persuasion. — — —

(b) When a salesman tries to persuade me to buy something, I decide for myself whether I really need or want it. — — —

(c) When my friend tries to persuade me to go to a party when I would rather stay home, I say no. — — —

15. *Responding to Failure:* Figuring out how and why you failed in a particular situation and what you can do about it in order to be more successful in the future.

(a) If I give a party and find that a few of my guests didn't enjoy themselves, I don't blame myself. — — —

(b) If I invite a friend to go someplace with me and get turned down, I don't give up my plans. — — —

(c) If I don't get a job after an employment interview, I don't become too discouraged. — — —

	1	2	3
	Always or Almost Always	Sometimes	Hardly Ever or Never

16. *Responding to Contradictory Messages:*
Recognizing and dealing with the con-
fusion that results when others tell you
one thing, but say or do things that indicate
that they mean something else.
    (a) When my friends say that they really
        had a good time with me and then turn
        down my suggestion that we get to-
        gether again, I point out the contradic-
        tion and ask for an explanation.   ___ ___ ___
    (b) When my spouse says that he or she
        doesn't mind my getting home late and
        then complains about having to eat
        dinner alone, I let him or her know that
        this confuses me.   ___ ___ ___
    (c) If I don't get a job after having been
        told that my qualifications were satisfac-
        tory, I ask the employer to explain his
        decision.   ___ ___ ___

17. *Responding to a Complaint:* Trying to
arrive at a fair solution to someone's justified complaint.
    (a) I listen openly and respond to my

	1	2	3
	Always or Almost Always	Sometimes	Hardly Ever or Never

spouse's complaint about my buying something that he or she thought was unnecessary.   ___ ___ ___

(b) When my boss becomes angry about a detail I've overlooked, I respond calmly and rationally, without becoming sullen.   ___ ___ ___

(c) When my neighbor nastily complains about a problem I'm causing, I listen and take appropriate action about the problem.   ___ ___ ___

18. *Concentrating on a Task:* Making those preparations that will help you get a job done efficiently.

(a) I work on a task without being easily distracted by other activities going on around me.   ___ ___ ___

(b) I concentrate on a task that must be done even if it doesn't particularly interest me.   ___ ___ ___

(c) I concentrate on a task without being distracted by thinking about other things that I must do later in the day.   ___ ___ ___

	1	2	3
	Always or Almost Always	Sometimes	Hardly Ever or Never

19. *Preparing for a Stressful Conversation:* Planning what you think will be the most effective presentation of your point of view.
    - (a) I can summon the courage for a difficult conversation with my neighbor. ___ ___ ___
    - (b) I prepare myself for a stressful encounter with my spouse. ___ ___ ___
    - (c) When I have to talk about difficult emotional family matters, I prepare myself for the conversation. ___ ___ ___

20. *Making a Decision:* Deciding on realistic plans that you feel will be in your best interest.
    - (a) After listening to all sides of an issue, I then make my own decision about what to do. ___ ___ ___
    - (b) I realistically decide how much money I can afford to spend on a new car. ___ ___ ___
    - (c) I make decisions that are in my own best interest. ___ ___ ___

21. *Determining Responsibility:* Finding out

	1	2	3
	Always or Almost Always	Sometimes	Hardly Ever or Never

whether an event has been caused by circumstances within your control.

(a) I can determine who or what is responsible for a particular problem at work. ———

(b) I decide whether I have been the cause
of an argument. ———

(c) I figure out why I'm in a bad mood. ———

22. *Using Self-Control:* Controlling your temper so that things don't get out of hand.

(a) I control my temper when my children
disobey my requests. ———

(b) I control my temper when my spouse
does something that annoys me. ———

(c) I control my temper when a salesman
treats me rudely in a store. ———

23. *Negotiating:* Arriving at a plan that satisfies
both you and another person who has taken
a different position.

(a) I negotiate with repairmen on a fair
price for a job. ———

(b) When my spouse and I have family
problems, we compromise on a solution
we can both agree on. ———

	1	2	3
	Always or Almost Always	Sometimes	Hardly Ever or Never

(c) I negotiate with my friend when each of us wants to do something different. ___ ___ ___

24. *Being Assertive:* Standing up for yourself by letting people know what you want, how you feel, or what you think about something.

(a) I speak up when my boss asks me to do something just as I'm about to leave. ___ ___ ___

(b) When a friend asks a favor I would rather not grant, I'm able to say no. ___ ___ ___

(c) I cancel a social engagement if I decide that I don't want to go. ___ ___ ___

Use the next two pages to keep a listing of your skill strengths and weaknesses. Let's take a look at your strengths first. Go back through the questionnaire and find those skills for which you checked either column 1 (Always or Almost Always) or column 2 (Sometimes). Make a list of those skills in the spaces provided under the heading "Skill Name."

You may already be wondering why we suggest listing the skills that give you little or no trouble. People frequently emphasize those aspects of themselves that are problematic and tend to forget about the things they do well. Although

Skill Name

_____

_____

_____

_____

_____

_____

_____

_____

_____

_____

_____

_____

_____

_____

_____

_____

_____

this book is basically about improving your skillfulness in troublesome areas, we would like you to keep a balanced picture of yourself in mind.

Look over your list of skill strengths. Think about how you might be able to capitalize on the areas in which you are most competent. Are there situations in which you *could* use your skill strengths but instead focus on those aspects of the situation that demand a less familiar or more difficult skill? We would suggest that you use your current skill strengths as the groundwork for your skill-building program. As you attempt to use new skills, which will feel somewhat awkward at first, you can use your well-practiced, firmly established skills as a backup.

Now let's turn to your problem skills. Go back through your questionnaire a second time and find the items for which you checked column three (Hardly Ever or Never). These items show you which skills you find troublesome and may need to work on. Make a list of your problem skills in the first column of the spaces on the next page. Most people can find at least five to ten skills that they feel merit some improvement or polishing. In the second column, next to each skill, list the skills in terms of their importance to you. For instance, if the skills of "Listening," "Negotiating," and "Expressing Anger" appeared on your list, you would think about which of these skills, if added to your present collection of skills, was most important in increasing your personal satisfaction or interpersonal effectiveness. If the skill was "Listening," you would rank that skill number one (by putting a 1 next to it under *Importance*). If "Expressing Anger" was more urgent or more problematic than "Negotiating," you would rank "Expressing Anger" number two and "Negotiating" number three.

In the third column, next to each skill, we would like you to rate each skill in terms of its difficulty. Place one plus

Skill Name	Importance	Difficulty (+/++/+++)
_____	_____	_____
_____	_____	_____
_____	_____	_____
_____	_____	_____
_____	_____	_____
_____	_____	_____
_____	_____	_____
_____	_____	_____
_____	_____	_____
_____	_____	_____
_____	_____	_____
_____	_____	_____
_____	_____	_____
_____	_____	_____
_____	_____	_____
_____	_____	_____
_____	_____	_____

sign (+) next to each skill that you consider reasonably easy to work on or learn. Place two plus signs (++) next to those skills that you consider to be of medium difficulty. Place three plus signs (+++) next to the most difficult skills, or those that you feel will require a lot of effort to learn well. In the next chapter, we will teach you how to choose which of these skills to work on first and how to prepare to master the skill most effectively.

3

Getting Ready: Preparing to Change Your Behavior

Now that you've filled out your Skill Questionnaire, you should have a pretty clear idea of your skill strengths and weaknesses. Let's take that important information and begin to work with it. Toward that end, this chapter will help you prepare to improve the skill behaviors you wish to change. To maximize your chances of success, there are three steps we strongly urge you to follow. They are: (1) selecting a skill you want to change, (2) writing behavior-change contracts, and (3) getting the help and support of others. In order to help you succeed in using these three procedures, we'll describe each one in detail.

SELECTING A SKILL

You should choose with care the first skill you decide to tackle. Not only will you be learning the skill, but this will be the first time you use the behavior-change methods described in this book. Look at your Skill Questionnaire results. In choosing the first skill to learn or improve upon, don't pick an especially difficult one. If possible, select one you have rated +, or relatively easy to learn. Selecting a particularly difficult skill first may make your chances of success too small. Don't hesitate to pick one that's important to you, one that you have ranked high in terms of skill importance. That is, be sure to choose a skill you are truly motivated to learn. So, a skill you have ranked 1, 2, or 3 in importance, and have rated + in terms of difficulty, would be an ideal skill with which to start.

WRITING
BEHAVIOR-CHANGE CONTRACTS

A contract is a written agreement that states what skill-improvement goals you must reach in order to receive a particular reward. A great deal of psychological research shows that contracting can be a powerful tool in your attempts to change your behavior. After all, in one way or another, a great deal of what we do is for some type of payoff or reward, whether the reward is money, praise, satisfaction, or something else. It has been shown that your behavior will indeed change if you are rewarded for doing so, and if the reward follows the changed behavior as quickly as possible. No behavior change, no reward. There's nothing startling here. The Christmas bonus an employer gives for work done well, or the lunch that a friend takes you out for after you've helped him out of a jam are examples of the behavior-reward relationship just described. What's novel in what we're about to describe is that behavior change can and does occur when people write contracts with themselves. Yes, contracting is an important and effective part of improving a skill and making an effort to change your behavior even when you are the only person involved and the contract is with yourself. All you need to do is stick with the following contracting rules. Every contract should include, in writing:

1. A behavior-change goal

This should clearly and specifically describe the skill behaviors you plan to change. In Chapter 5, we've broken down each skill listed in your Skill Questionnaire into the behavioral steps that make it up. You should include these specific steps in the goal of your contract. In addition to spelling out *what* your behavior-change goal is (the steps that make up the skill), your contract should also include *where, when,* and *with whom* you plan to use the skill. You should contract with yourself to change only one skill at a time. Final goals, as well as intermediate or sub-goals, can be included in your contract. For instance, if your final goal is to be able to easily start a conversation at a party, a sub-goal might include starting a conversation with a co-worker at lunch.

2. Rewards

This should clearly and specifically describe the rewards you will provide yourself if you reach your behavior-change goal. These can include things you will *do* for yourself, such as seeing a special movie, buying a special item of clothing, or going to a special restaurant, and things you will *say* to yourself, e.g., "well done," "good job," etc. Be sure to also be specific about *when* you will reward yourself. The timing of rewards is crucial. In general, try to see to it that you are rewarded as soon as possible after you've used the skill. You should specify rewards for achieving your final goal as well as rewards for living up to intermediate goals. In the example of starting a conversation, you might buy yourself a small treat and say "Good job" to yourself after each time you start a conversation with a co-worker. After achieving your final goal, you might treat yourself to dinner at your favorite restaurant.

Another important principle that you should be aware of in setting up a program for rewarding yourself is to make sure you are generous in your rewards as you begin in your behavior-change efforts. It is particularly difficult to keep a behavior-change program going in its initial stages, since many of your efforts may feel awkward or uncomfortable. So reward yourself often and generously at first. Give yourself a pat on the back as you follow through on each step of your plan.

3. Negative consequences

This part of your contract should clearly and specifically describe the negative consequences you will give yourself if you fail to reach your behavior-change goal. These can include withholding either special (see above) or routine pleasures (TV, dessert, etc.); doing unpleasant household or other chores you've been putting off; contributing money to political or other causes *opposite* to those you actually believe in; and saying things to yourself like "I did a lousy job that time," "I didn't do well," etc. You will find it particularly tempting to abandon your behavior-change program the first time you fail to live up to your goal. Don't give up. Give yourself a negative consequence, and move on ahead.

4. Bonuses

The contract should clearly and specifically describe the bonus rewards you will give yourself if you exceed your behavior-change goal. Such rewards can be the same as those previously described, but in greater quantity. Or, bonus rewards can be even more special things you can do for yourself. It is often a good policy to plan on giving yourself the smaller rewards described above for each step of progress you make, and a special or bonus reward when the skill learning and use in tough, real-life situations are completed. The bonus rewards will be especially appropriate if you do better than you planned, or complete the learning of the skill earlier than you planned.

5. Record-keeping

Your contract should include a clear and specific description of how you can keep track of your progress in learning and improving the skill behaviors. Sometimes it may be hard to judge when you are making progress in learning a skill. You may have a general feeling that you are or are not moving ahead but may not be sure. Avoid such uncertainty; it will definitely interfere with proper use of your contract and satisfactory skill improvement. If it's at all possible, we suggest you keep a record of how well or how poorly you used a skill in various situations. Start this record a week or two *before* you begin using Structured Learning (to see where you are starting from). Keep the record during your self-training (to judge your progress), and also record your skill use for a couple of weeks after training (to be sure where you have ended up, and whether you're hanging on to what you've learned). This record-keeping, or, as it is sometimes called, "self-monitoring," can be done on a tally sheet you put up on a closet door, on a card you carry with you, by means of a golf wrist counter, or in similar ways. It also helps to have a friend or relative whom you trust and with whom you spend a lot of time help you in recording your skill improvement. If your use of the methods described in this book goes well, your record-keeping tally sheet for your good skill use might look like this:

BEFORE STRUCTURED LEARNING		DURING STRUCTURED LEARNING		AFTER STRUCTURED LEARNING	
Week 1		Week 2	Week 3	Week 4	Week 5
S	I	III	III	ⅡⅡⅡ	ⅡⅡⅡ
M	II	ⅡⅡⅡ	ⅡⅡⅡ	ⅡⅡⅡ	ⅡⅡⅡ
Tu	I	II	III	III	ⅡⅡⅡ
W	ⅡⅡⅡ	ⅡⅡⅡ I	ⅡⅡⅡ	ⅡⅡⅡ I	ⅡⅡⅡ
Th	I	III	ⅡⅡⅡ	ⅡⅡⅡ	III
F	I	II	III	ⅡⅡⅡ	ⅡⅡⅡ
S		I	III	III	III

Let's look at an example of a behavior-change contract. (Additional examples of behavior-change contracts appear later in the book.) In Chapter 1, we briefly met Paul Johnson, timid, unassertive, growing more and more unhappy with himself and increasingly dissatisfied with being left behind (socially and financially) at work. Paul would like a raise and the recognition that goes with it (a long-range goal). But he realizes that he's a long way from asking his boss for a raise. In fact, Paul seldom initiates conversations with anyone at work (let alone asking for a raise!), but rather waits for others to talk to him. Paul decides that a reasonable goal to begin with is to start more conversations with people at work. Using this goal, he's ready to write his behavior-change contract.

Before beginning, he decides to keep track of how often he actually starts conversations at work. He chooses a typical work week as a test period and records a tally on his desk calendar for each conversation he begins. During his test period, he discovers that he's only started one conversation. Paul then writes his contract (see page 40).

For your use in contract writing, five blank contract forms appear at the end of this book.

GETTING HELP FROM OTHERS

There is an excellent chance that you'll learn to use the skill behaviors effectively if you have chosen a skill that is important to you and, in your first few tries, is not very difficult; if you have written a reasonable behavior-change contract with yourself for this skill; and if you follow the specific behavior-change procedures described in the next chapter. The chances of behavior change will be even greater, however, if you are able to enlist the help of other people in your skill-improvement efforts. This should include one or more people whom you feel you can trust—a friend, relative, co-worker, etc. If such a person is available to be of aid, we suggest you ask him to help in as many of the following ways as are appropriate:

1. Discuss your behavior-change plans with the person. Even if this discussion only results in the other person's knowing your plan and goal, with no request for him or her to do anything, you have made an open and "public" com-

BEHAVIOR-CHANGE CONTRACT

Behavior-Change Goal: Initiate at least one conversation each day at work.

Behavioral Steps to be Followed:

1. Choose the right place and time.

2. Greet the other people.

3. Make small talk.

4. Judge if the other person is listening and wants to talk.

5. Open with the main topic I want to

X. talk about, and do it with Kim (next desk),

X. Sid (mail room), John (purchasing), Sally (reception), or Joanne (boss's secretary).

Reward: Buy myself a dessert and say "I'm doing well" after I've achieved my goal for that day.

Negative Consequences: No dessert and no TV at night for each day I have not achieved my goal.

Bonus: Buy a new tie if 100% successful for two weeks; say "I'm really doing well. I'm proud of myself!"

Record-Keeping: Continue to keep tallies on my desk calendar.

Beginning Date: April 29 _____ Ending Date: May 13

Signature: Paul Johnson

mitment of sorts. We have even worked with some individuals who declared their commitment to learning a given skill by posting a notice on a closet door! Once others know what you're trying to accomplish, it becomes more likely that you'll make a serious effort at it.

2. Ask others for support and responsiveness. You can, and probably should, go beyond just telling others what *you* plan to do. It will often be helpful, in addition, to ask for their help in specific ways. Sometimes the help may be passive, such as asking them not to interfere or interrupt when you're trying your new skill. For example, if something is wrong with your meal in a restaurant and you wish to use the skill "Expressing a Complaint," ask your spouse not to interfere while you complain. Or, you may ask him or her to take a more active role in helping, such as letting you know when you've used the skill well or when you've used it poorly. In the example we described above, after you've expressed the complaint, your spouse could tell you how well you followed the behavioral steps of that skill, whether you were too aggressive or too apologetic, and whether you were effective in the results you got. You often should go even further and request that when you use the skill you're working on, you would like the other person to respond in a particular way. For example, when you're practicing the skill "Expressing a Compliment," the other person should respond with correct "listening" behaviors; when you are trying to resolve a disagreement by "Negotiating," the person helping you should also negotiate; and so forth.

3. Write a contract with someone. Earlier in this chapter we described a set of steps you should use when writing effective behavior-change contracts with yourself. Contracts also can be (and usually are) written between two people. A very desirable way for you to seek help from others is by asking them to contract with you. Your role in the contract

is to use the new skill. The other person's role is mainly to control the payoff for reaching your goal. In other words, your helper controls the rewards, giving them if you're successful or withholding them if you're not. Remember, though, you are the person ultimately responsible for your success or failure. Be careful not to fall into the trap of blaming your helper when progress is difficult. If you use your skill especially well, the helper gives you both the reward you contracted for and the bonus reward. And if your efforts fail, that person delivers the negative consequences you've spelled out in the contract. Your helper can also help you decide what skill to work on, where and when you might try to use it, how to observe and record your progress, and what rewards and negative consequences should be contracted for.

This chapter has had three purposes. We have shown you how to select a skill to work on from those that your Skill Questionnaire showed you needed to work on. We've described the specific steps involved in writing a behavior-change contract with yourself so that you increase your chances of learning your skill effectively. And we've suggested ways you can get the help and support of others to aid you in this learning. Once you have completed these three preparation steps, you're ready to actually learn the skill you've chosen. In the next chapter we'll talk about how you can do this.

4

What to Do About It:
Changing
Your Behavior

You've prepared yourself for learning new behavioral skills. You've chosen the skill deficiencies you want to change. You've written your behavior-change contract and you've arranged for someone else to help you. Now it's time to look at *how* you can learn the skill behaviors rapidly and well. The method we will describe for doing this we call *Structured Learning.* Several dozen psychological studies have shown how effective Structured Learning is as a method for developing skills. This research has evaluated and established its success with many types of persons—business managers, hospital employees, adult psychotherapy patients, police officers, parents, clergymen, adolescents, and others.

All aspects of Structured Learning share two qualities crucial in developing new skills. First, it is *behavioral.* While we hope (and expect) that using Structured Learning will lead to positive changes in your attitudes toward yourself (self-confidence, self-respect, sense of worth, or competence), the direct goal is *behavior change.* Many self-help procedures ask you to work on your self-attitudes, to befriend yourself, to respect yourself, to "pull yourself up by your bootstraps." Unfortunately, even when some change in self-attitude occurs, behavior change rarely follows. And, when attitude change fails to make a difference in what you actually *do,* the attitude change itself tends to fade away. When you don't see yourself *doing* things in a more competent or satisfying manner, there is no reason to continue to feel better about yourself. However, matters are very different the other way around. If you can succeed in developing new skills, in actually behaving differently—more effectively, competently, satisfyingly—positive changes in your attitudes about yourself almost certainly follow. Just think for a moment about how you felt about yourself when you learned a new skill and used it well . . . with a member of the opposite sex, or with your boss, or your children or a friend, at work, or on a tennis court, or in the workshop, or at home. When you *do* something well, you *feel good* about yourself. In short, self-attitude change only very rarely leads to behavior change, but behavior change very often results in self-attitude change. Therefore, all the procedures that make up Structured Learning are procedures aimed at changing your behavior first, with the expectation that your feelings and attitudes about yourself also will change—for the better.

Structured Learning is not only behavioral, it is also an *active* learning method. We all see or read about things every day—on TV, on films, or in books and newspapers—that are good examples of how a skill can be used well, but we fail to do likewise. Why? Because passive learning (that is, just watching someone on TV or just reading about a socially effective person) is often simply not powerful enough instruction. To learn something well, especially if it's a skill that has caused us a lot of difficulty in the past, the learning process has to be an active and involving one. Observing or reading tells us *what* to do; being actively involved (rehearsing or practicing the skill) teaches us more fully *how* to do it. We need both for effective and lasting learning. It is for this reason that Structured Learning is an active learning method.

Structured Learning consists of four procedures: (1)

describing the behavior, (2) rehearsing the behavior, (3) getting feedback on the behavior, and (4) transferring the behavior. We'll explain each procedure and tell you how you can use it effectively for developing skills.

BEHAVIORAL DESCRIPTION

Each of the skills listed on your Skill Questionnaire (including those you've chosen as your behavior-change goals) can be broken down into the specific behaviors, or steps, that make up the skill. We've broken down each of the Skill Questionnaire skills in this way, and the behavioral descriptions appear in the following chapter. For any skill described there, if you do the steps presented in the order presented, you will have used that skill effectively. From our behavioral point of view, the behavioral steps *are* the skill. We are not suggesting that the behavioral steps we feel should make up any given skill are the *only* good way to use that skill. Instead, we feel the steps are one good way and therefore we recommend them. Obviously, if you find that adding steps of your own, dropping some, or using different steps is effective for you, do it. But if you are having trouble with a skill, the steps we've suggested remain a good starting point, at minimum, and very often will continue to be the most effective way for you to use the skill.

Thus, once your goal, contract, and help from others are set, your next step is to turn to Chapter 5 and read the behavioral description of the skill you've decided to work on. Read, study, write down, and memorize the steps that make up the skill, and read and think about the brief stories presented after each description. These sketches are illustrations of both good and poor use of the skill. Obviously, we urge you to focus on good skill use to help guide you in *your* use of the steps, and to focus on poor skill use to help you be aware of and avoid the pitfalls and problems you may meet when trying to use the skill.

BEHAVIORAL REHEARSAL

We stressed earlier that Structured Learning requires you to *actively* train yourself so that effective and lasting learning may occur. Of course, you may be able to learn and use some skills simply by reading the skills' descriptions. But remember, this book seeks to help you learn skills that have been difficult or impossible for you in the past. For most of these skills, passive reading of what to do probably won't be enough. Rehearsing the behavior is one excellent way for you to become actively involved in learning the skill.

Behavioral rehearsal allows you to practice a skill's steps in such a manner that you gradually become more and more skillful in using it in the real-life situations in which you need it. The key here is gradualness. It is important that you be certain to practice the skill in easier situations before moving on to more difficult situations. We suggest you use the following gradual sequence to practice the behavioral steps for the skill you have selected.

1. In imagination

Think about the various situations in which you'd like to use the target skill. Pick one and picture yourself in that setting. Imagine where it is, when you might be there, and who is likely to be there with you. Imagine yourself going through the behavioral steps in the correct order and with no errors. Let the entire sequence unfold as smoothly as you can. Imagine not only what you would think, say, or do, but also what the other people involved might say or do in response to you.

2. Openly, alone

Now go through the correct behavioral-step sequence again, but this time say aloud what you might actually say and do in the real-life skill situation. Even if it feels a bit strange to do, try to make your words, expressions, gestures, and movements as real and as relevant as you can. Make it a true *behavioral* rehearsal. For reasons we will discuss below, in order to get feedback on your performance, we urge you in this step of rehearsal to use a mirror and, if available, a tape recorder.

3. Openly, with someone you trust

Let's assume your skill goal is "Expressing Anger." Your intention is to develop this skill to a point at which you can express justifiable anger to, for example, a co-worker who has frequently treated you unfairly. You have practiced the behavioral steps that make up "Expressing Anger" both in your imagination, and aloud in front of a mirror, using a tape recorder. In the third stage of behavioral rehearsal, a second person becomes involved. This is your chance to go through the steps again, but this time do it while looking someone else in the eyes, responding to their comebacks. In this first attempt with someone else, the other person should, if possible, be a person you trust and who will cooperate. Often it's wise to pick a person like the one we described on pages 39 to 42 under the topic "Getting Help from Others." First, describe what skill you want to practice and why you would like help. Give your helper all the details you can about the real-life situation in which you eventually want to use the skill—where, when, why, and with which real-life target person. Tell him all about the person to whom you want to express your feelings of anger . . . the individual's name, appearance, characteristics, and, most important, what response this target person is likely to have to you. Tell the person helping you to imitate the other person's behavior as closely as possible while you practice the skill. This is a rehearsal. It's designed to teach you a skill for use where, when, and with whom you really need it. The more realistic the rehearsal, the better your real-life skill behavior will be. It often will be useful to repeat this rehearsal a number of times, until you feel fully comfortable using your new skill behavior.

4. Openly, with the real-life target person

Your final stage is to use the skill with the actual people in the actual places, where it counts. In using your newly learned skill behaviors at work, at home, in social situations, and elsewhere, gradually work up to using them with your target people. If it is easier for you, take on a co-worker before trying the skill with your boss. Try other skills out with people who are more cooperative before you deal with those who are less cooperative. Use the skill in less difficult situations before you tackle the really tough ones. Challenge yourself, but do it gradually!

BEHAVIORAL FEEDBACK

You have studied a skill and tried it out both alone and with one or more people. It's important now to determine how well you're doing. Are you carrying out the behavioral steps correctly? Are you doing them in the proper order? Could you do it better? Are you doing well in some situations but still having difficulty in others? Why aren't you getting the results you expected? Feedback on questions like these is crucial to your progress. With adequate feedback, you can eliminate errors and sharpen your skill performance. Without such feedback, your skill deficiency may remain unchanged, without your ever understanding why a particular situation never turns out the way you'd like it to.

You can provide yourself with behavioral feedback during the first two rehearsal stages ("In imagination" and "Openly, alone"). Use your mirror and tape recorder to honestly help you judge whether the words, expressions, gestures, and movements of your rehearsal actually fit the skill's behavioral steps. When you shift to rehearsal with someone you trust, ask that person the same questions: Am I following the steps? How do I look and sound? Do I look natural and comfortable using the skill? Can you suggest anything I might improve upon?

There is another type of feedback your helper can give you, and it's very important feedback indeed. The behavioral steps that make up all of the skills in Chapter 5 are designed to be effective means for solving whatever problem is involved. The goal in designing the steps for "Expressing Anger," for example, was not just to make you feel better (or to "get it out of your system") but especially to maximize the chances that the person you confront will respond to you as you wish (an apology, correcting an error he or she has made, etc.). That is, often the most important feedback we can get is *results*. Did it work? Did I accomplish my goal in using the skill behavior? You can get approximate answers to such questions during the rehearsal process by asking the person helping you to react to your skill rehearsal just the way the actual target person would react. If you've set up the rehearsal well, you've told your helper a great deal about the target person and his or her typical reactions. Having your helper try to *be* that person, especially in reacting to your behavior, can often provide especially valuable feedback. In the example we have been using, if your helper feels your expression of anger would result in an apology, he or she should apologize. If your helper feels it would lead to counter-anger toward you, he or she should express anger. Urge your helper to provide you with whatever real-life reaction seems most likely. Only then can you evaluate your progress realistically, and prepare adequately for real-life encounters.

It is, of course, the feedback from the real-life people themselves that ultimately tests how adequate and competent your skill behavior has been. If, in general (there may always be exceptions), people in your world are responding to you as you would like, you're probably using your skills effectively. If, on the other hand, many of your skill trials yield unsatisfying or ineffective results, there's an excellent chance that you need to work more on developing those skills. Be quite sure, however, when evaluating any negative feedback or results you receive, to discover what caused the negative results. Were you using your skills ineffectively? Or was it the case that the other person was unreceptive, stubborn, or lacking in skills? It's true that there will be some times when even though you've done your best, others may not respond quite as you hoped they would. In general, however, using a skill effectively will most often lead to rewarding outcomes.

BEHAVIORAL TRANSFER

The methods we've just described will very likely help you learn the skills you select. Unfortunately, it's too often true that you can either forget or not use your newly learned skills where and when it counts. That is, you may become very skilled at being assertive or expressing an apology or asking for help during behavioral rehearsal, but not do well when you wish to be assertive toward your real boss, apologize to your real wife, or ask actual strangers for help. This is the problem of behavioral transfer. The question is, will your ability to perform the skill transfer from where and when you learned it to where and when you need it in real life? This is an all-important matter because if behavioral transfer is too weak, the entire skill-training program was largely a waste of time and effort. Behavioral transfer is so important that we've devoted an entire chapter to it (Chapter 6). In that chapter we'll give you a series of steps you can take to increase the chances that *your* skill learning will transfer to the actual situations in which you need your skills.

5

*Personal Skills
in Action:
Guidelines,
Steps,
and Examples*

This chapter is a cookbook of sorts. On the following pages you'll find information about all the skills included in your Skill Questionnaire. (Chapter 7, *More Personal Skills,* provides behavioral steps for a number of additional skills. Although these additional skills do not appear on the Skill Questionnaire [since they are troublesome to somewhat fewer persons than those examined in this chapter], they are a problem for some people, some of the time, and therefore they are included as a supplement.) Each skill is broken down into a series of behavioral steps. We've done this in order to help you learn and practice the specific behaviors that make up that skill. Just as you can make a complex problem more manageable by breaking it down into its parts, you can make each skill more learnable by breaking it down into its behavioral steps. You will note that some of the steps of a particular skill may be things that you do or say. Other steps may be things that you think or decide.

   After the set of steps that make up each skill, you'll find a story demonstrating how someone else has learned to use that skill effectively. These stories are meant to serve, therefore, as examples of good use of the skill. The numbers inserted are there to show you which behavioral step is being used at that time. You will be able to see how the steps flow together to make up the skill.

Certainly these examples represent only one way of skillfully solving a particular problem. You may be able to find other good examples of effective skill use before you begin your own practice or skill-improvement plan. Try to think about people who are skillful in using the particular skill on which you're working. Just like our stories, these people may also serve as good models for you. Watch them closely. Notice the steps they use in carrying out a skill. You'll find that they very often use some or all of the steps listed here. They may, however, have found other effective solutions to the problem. As we've said before, the steps listed here represent good, proven ways of improving your skillfulness, but are not the only good ways.

While each of the stories in this chapter is an example of effective use of the behavioral steps that make up a skill, each is also something more. Remember, you should read and use this book as a total behavior-change program. The *preparation* procedures described in Chapter 3 are there to prepare you to learn the skills in this chapter. The Structured Learning procedures in Chapter 4 are the *learning* methods for these same skills. And Chapter 6, which describes *transfer* procedures, will help make the skills you've learned lasting ones. Because these preparation, learning, and transfer procedures are all so vital to your skill learning, many of the examples that follow also illustrate the use of these behavior-change procedures. That is, each story gives an example of good use of a skill plus an example of one or more procedures of the preparation–learning–transfer sequence described in other chapters.

We know that how good or poor you are in a given skill will vary. In some instances, you may be pretty good at the skill already but still desire some brushing up. To learn such skills you may only need to read examples of good skill use and then try the skills' steps out yourself. The stories for Skills 2, 7, 15, 22, and 24 show people attempting to use skills this way—by reading and doing. There may be other skills in which you are moderately deficient. You have had some success at them, but not very much. For these skills, your preparation, learning, and transfer efforts will have to be more energetic, and go well beyond just reading and trying. You will, instead, probably have to make effective use of several of the preparation, learning, and transfer procedures we've described in other chapters. To help you in this effort, we've provided in the examples that follow (besides examples of good skill use) examples of contracting (Skills 3, 4, and 9), getting help from others (Skills 9, 14, 17, and 21), using behavioral rehearsal with yourself or with others (Skills 1, 11, 12, and 17), and obtaining behavioral feedback (Skill 10). For those skills in which you have very little ability or none at all, skills in which you are essentially starting from scratch, we urge you to use *all* the procedures described in Chapters 3, 4, and 6. You will need *full* attention to all aspects of preparation, Structured Learning, and transfer. Skill 23 is an example of this complete set's being used effectively.

SKILL 1: Starting a Conversation

Steps in starting a conversation:

[1] Choose the right place and time.

[2] Greet the other person.

[3] Make small talk.

[4] Judge if the person is listening and wants to talk with you.

[5] Open the main topic you want to talk about.

● **Ann Thomas's Self-Diagnosis.** I really have a problem with parties. I look forward to going, spend hours getting ready, arrive with a feeling of anticipation and excitement (while trying to appear very cool), and then as the evening progresses, I slowly fade into the woodwork. Usually I make some excuse to leave early. When I leave, I try to look bored or aloof—I don't want to be too conspicuous. I've thought about it and what's really going on is that I'm afraid to meet new people. I worry that they won't like me, or that they'll laugh at me, or that they'll be bored and leave me standing in the middle of the room with my mouth open. The result is that I wind up sitting in some corner, eating too much food, and watching everybody else have a good time. When I go home, I manage to feel very sorry for myself, and spend hours looking in the mirror thinking about why I'm so unpopular. When I finally sit back and try to analyze the problem rationally, I realize that what I've been doing is counting on other people to notice me and talk to me (even when I'm sitting in a corner), rather than taking the initiative to start conversations with them.

Skill Use: What I'd like to be able to do, eventually, is to go to parties, start conversations with people there, and, especially, meet new people without putting myself down or feeling so nervous. I decided that before I was ready to tackle a party situation, I needed to get some practice starting conversations in situations where I felt less nervous in general. It also occurred to me that I could practice starting conversations with people I knew as acquaintances before walking up to total strangers. I decided to use the cafeteria at work as my practice laboratory. I planned that at every lunchtime, for two weeks, I'd have my lunch with the regular crowd. I'd make a point of being the person to start the conversation, rather than letting others start the ball rolling, as I usually do.

After two weeks of practice in following the steps for starting a conversation at work, first awkwardly and later quite successfully, and doing it well, I finally felt ready to tackle the real problem. The opportunity came when my friend Julie invited me to a pizza party she was planning. I decided that I'd go and I'd start a conversation with at least one new person there. I was aware that the conversation might turn out to be a total bust, particularly with someone I didn't know. But I figured I'd give it my best try and see what would happen. When I arrived I realized that the only person I knew there was Julie. I did notice, though, that there was a guy who was in my evening English class. He seemed like a good target for me to practice on. [1] I waited until he was finished talking with some people, and walked over as he was cutting a piece of pizza for himself. [2] I said "Hi" and asked him if he would cut a piece of pizza for me. He smiled and said, "Sure." So far, so good. As he was cutting the pizza, I introduced myself and asked him his name. [3] We sat down and began eating, and I commented on how good the pizza was. [4] He seemed friendly and relaxed, so I figured he was interested in continuing the conversation. [5] I mentioned that I'd seen him in English class, and that I was putting in a lot of time on the term paper we had due at the end of the month. I told him a bit about my paper, and then asked him what he was writing about. We continued talking for about ten minutes, and then some friends of his came over. He introduced me and we all started talking. I felt pleased with myself. I'd done what I set out to do, and there was a good payoff. I wound up meeting four new people that evening, and I left for home without that gloomy, depressed feeling I usually have.

SKILL 2: Ending a Conversation

Steps in ending a conversation:

[1] Summarize the other person's and your main topic.
[2] Draw a conclusion.
[3] Ask for the other person's reaction.
[4] Respond to the other person's reaction.
[5] Make a closing remark.

● **Bill Dulany's Self-Diagnosis.** Have you ever felt as if you were trapped into talking with someone and just couldn't end the conversation? Well, it happens to me a lot, particularly at parties. I find myself talking with people long after I've exhausted anything I might want to talk about. Sometimes I would rather not socialize than be caught being unable to break off a conversation when I wanted to.

Thinking about the problem a bit more, I realized that I generally didn't have that difficulty at work. I could be very businesslike and move from one scheduled appointment to the next. Not so at social gatherings, however. I decided that I really needed some help in dealing more comfortably with ending conversations in social situations.

Skill Use: My first step in working on ending conversations was to read through the steps, and to think about particular times when I've had trouble ending a conversation. The first thing that came to mind was the annual summer cocktail party that our good friends the Collinses had. I get along well enough with Nick Collins, but once he gets on the topic of golf—which he talks about all summer long—there's no stopping him. When we got the invitation a few weeks ago, I told my wife, Margaret, that maybe we should make some excuse and not go this year because I couldn't avoid talking to Nick, and I couldn't bear the thought of another endless golf saga. But Margaret really wanted to go, so we accepted. The question then became: How am I going to end that inevitable conversation with Nick? After thinking about my last encounter, I tried to figure out how I might have ended it by using the steps. First I thought it through ("He would say '——,' then I would say '——,'"), and then I actually rehearsed it out loud. After a couple of times, I was actually feeling a little more in control. The test would be the party, however, and Nick's inevitable stories.

Sure enough, ten minutes after we had arrived at the Collinses', Nick had me trapped in the corner, talking about a new golf course he had tried. As soon as he started, however, I made a point of saying that I was planning to play more tennis this summer. Nick went on for a couple more minutes and I was beginning to get a little bored, so I made a serious effort to break it off smoothly. It went something like this:

Me: [1] "So Nick, it sounds like another full summer of golf for you. For me, I really like the running around you get with a fast set of tennis. [2] Say, if you have any interest in playing some tennis, give me a call. [3] What do you think?"

Nick: "No, I think I'll stick to my golf."

Me: [4] "Well, keep it in mind. [5] Good talking to you."

For the first time in a long time, I felt as if I'd kept control of the conversation and that I was able to end it without feeling too awkward. And I wasn't rude to Nick.

SKILL 3: Listening

Steps in listening:

[1] Look at the other person.
[2] Show your interest in that person's statement; e.g., nod your head, use appropriate body language, etc.
[3] Ask questions on the same topic.
[4] Add your thoughts and feelings on the topic.

● **Peggy Conn's Self-Diagnosis.** I had been so busy with my job, my school work, and all my regular household chores that I hadn't realized that Jimmy, my six-year-old, wasn't getting much of my attention. One evening about a month ago, while I was fixing dinner, I was aware of his little voice saying, "Mommy, you never listen to me." Later that evening, I did some thinking about what Jimmy had said. I realized that he was right—that I hadn't been listening to him much lately. I also began thinking about other recent times when I hadn't been a very good listener. It seemed that all those occasions with Jimmy, and at work, had something in common: When I became preoccupied with doing something or thinking about something, I just didn't pay much attention to those who wanted to talk to me. I decided that I really wasn't being fair to Jimmy, or to some of the people at work, so I decided it was time to try to do something about it.

Skill Use: After reviewing the steps for "Listening," I decided to set a behavior change goal for myself—to improve my listening skills. To do this, I realized, I would need to work on it, particularly in situations in which it is likely that I might be doing something else. So I made up a behavior-change contract with myself: that I would apply myself to better listening (following the steps) at least once a day, and I would keep a tally on the calendar in the kitchen. It wasn't so easy at first. I found that with Ted, my husband, I would start out listening and then drift off into what I wanted to talk about. I wound up doing some of Ted's usual chores quite a few times the first week (my negative consequence in my contract).

I stuck with my contract in spite of all the problems I was having with listening, and about three weeks later I began to see my practice start to pay off. For about a week, I had been relatively successful in listening to Jimmy when he asked for my attention. That particular day, when I got home from work, he greeted me with "Guess what happened at school today?" Instead of going on about the business of preparing dinner while only half attending to him, I put down my things and [1] sat down at the table and looked at him and I asked, "What?" As he proceeded with his story about a friend who had gotten hurt at school, [2] I gave him my undivided attention and responded to what he was saying by nodding and frowning and smiling at the right times. When he was done telling me about his friend's injury, [3] I asked him about the rest of his day and [4] then I told him I was sorry that his friend got hurt. Jimmy came over and gave me a big hug. It was so spontaneous and warm. I really feel a lot better about my listening behavior, particularly with Jimmy. Even in a few short weeks, our pre-dinner conversations have become a very rewarding routine.

SKILL 4: Expressing a Compliment

Steps in expressing a compliment:

[1] Decide what it is about the other person you want to compliment.

[2] Decide whether the other person would like to hear the compliment.

[3] Choose the right time and place to express the compliment.

[4] Express the compliment in a sincere and friendly manner.

● **Robert Jamison's Self-Diagnosis.** Oh, boy, it happened again last week, after I promised myself I wouldn't let it. I've always had trouble complimenting my wife, Sue. I feel awkward when it comes to saying something nice. She's been kind of depressed lately, and she's having a hard time keeping up with the kids and the work around the house. I know one of the things that gets her down in the dumps is my getting thoughtless and taking her for granted a lot of the time. I know that I should show my appreciation for all the things she does around the house, like cooking and taking such good care of the kids all day. I do appreciate what she does, but it's just hard to show it. I feel dumb with all this sentimental stuff. The members of my family never said nice things to one another. I guess that's why I'm the same way.

Well, I knew last week that it was time to make some changes. I wasn't about to have my wife feeling depressed because of one of my hangups.

Skill Use: I read through the steps for "Expressing a Compliment" and realized that my problem was to choose the right time and place to pay the compliment. Around our house, things are kind of hectic all day long. There's really no way to say anything sincerely without shouting over the noise or being interrupted by the phone or the doorbell. I decided that the best time to tell my wife how much I appreciated her was at night, after things had quieted down. What that meant was that I would have to keep track of the things she had done that day, so I could compliment her about real things she had done. I figured that a written contract would help not so much for rewards or that kind of stuff, but to help me keep track of how I was doing. [Robert's contract appears opposite.]

The week went pretty well. [1] On Monday, Sue cooked an especially good dinner. [2] I knew she'd like me to say something about it. [3] I decided to tell her during the first quiet moment I could find. [4] When the kids left the house to go over to a neighbor's after dinner, I let her know how much I enjoyed the meal and that I knew she worked hard to prepare it. She smiled and said, "Thanks." I did my homework and paid a compliment to Sue on five out of the seven days. I also sent $2.00 off to charity, since I had missed two days and had contracted to pay a penalty. I have given myself the same assignment for next week, with one small addition. I plan to compliment her by doing something nice for her at least once during the week.

SKILL 5: Asking for Help

Steps in asking for help:

[1] Decide what the problem is.

[2] Decide if you want help with the problem.

[3] Identify the people who might help you.

[4] Make a choice of helper.

[5] Tell the helper about your problem.

● **Karen Larson's Self-Diagnosis.** My high-school yearbook predicted that I would become a "fiercely independent career woman." You know, after almost ten years, that prediction has proven true, at least from outward appearances. Friends have actually told me how much they admire my self-reliance, appar-

BEHAVIOR-CHANGE CONTRACT

Behavior-Change Goal: to express a compliment to Sue
at least once a day for the work she does at home.

Behavioral Steps to be Followed:

1. Decide what it is about Sue I want to
   compliment
2. Decide whether she would like to hear it.
3. Choose the right time and place.
4. Express the compliment in a
5. sincere and friendly manner.
6. _____
7. _____

Reward: Sue's appreciation and her
improved spirits.

Negative Consequences: For every day I don't express a
compliment, I'll contribute $1 to my least-
favorite charity.

Bonus: If I compliment my wife at least
once a day for 3 weeks, I'll buy a new tie.

Record-Keeping: Keep track on my calendar.

Beginning Date: January 7th Ending Date: February 7th

Signature: Robert Jamieson

ent self-confidence, and success in a career that only a few years ago just about excluded women. And, to tell you the truth, I do feel pretty confident about my ability at work. What happens, however, is that I feel that I should be *totally* self-reliant—that people expect me, and I expect myself—to do everything myself, and never ask for help. When a problem comes up at work, I do my darndest to figure it out for myself. In some ways I guess that attitude has helped me—learning by doing, that is. On the other hand, I know it's kind of bullheaded. And to tell the truth, it's hard to ask for help. It makes me feel kind of vulnerable.

Where I have the most difficulty in asking for help involves my social life. Most of my women friends got married right after high school or college. They imagine that I have some kind of glamorous social life, with dates, travel, variety, romance. If they only knew! Sure, I date, but it's really very hard for me to meet men. It's particularly difficult when I feel that I have to keep up appearances for my friends and pretend that I'm perfectly content with the way things are. I've decided that continuing to keep up a front is silly, and that I really need to ask for some help with my social life.

Skill Use: My plan was rather simple, once I identified the steps for asking for help. And my attempt at solving the problem fell right into line with the steps. It went something like this:

[1] The problem was my lousy social life. I really needed some help in meeting new men. [2] Yes, reluctantly I realized that I wanted and needed to seek help for the problem, because my attempts to meet men on my own weren't working out. [3] I thought about whom I might turn to. The most logical place to begin seemed to be the women I had remained friendly with since high school days. Although they were all married, they probably did know some single men, through their husbands, jobs, clubs, or whatever. [4] After thinking through my list of friends, I decided that I would approach Linda. She's been a good friend over the years, and I felt that I would be most comfortable discussing my problem with her. Besides, she worked in an office and certainly had a lot of contacts. [5] Well, I asked Linda to meet me for lunch last Wednesday. Occasionally, we've had lunch together

downtown, so my invitation wasn't so out of the ordinary. We met at the restaurant, sat down at our table, and exchanged pleasantries. Then Linda said, "Well, tell me what's new in your exciting life."

Instead of my usual reply about all that I was doing, I said, "To tell you the truth, Linda, it's kind of lonely a lot of the time. I'm having a heck of a time meeting men that I'd be interested in dating. I was wondering if you might be able to help me."

"You're kidding!"

"No, Linda, it's the truth."

Linda said she didn't know of any interesting single men right off the bat, but that if I didn't mind she'd ask Jim, her husband, if he knew anyone. She said she was surprised to hear that my social life wasn't so hot and if she had known she'd have had an eye out for me for months.

Well, we talked about work and gardening and stuff for a while and before I knew it, it was time to go. Linda told me she'd call me next week sometime.

I don't know how my honesty will pay off in the long run, but I felt good about doing what I had set out to do—ask for help.

SKILL 6: Giving Instructions

Steps in giving instructions:

[1] Define what needs to be done and who should do it.

[2] Tell the other person what you want him or her to do, and why.

[3] Tell the other person exactly how to do what you want done.

[4] Ask for his or her reactions.

[5] Consider his or her reactions and change your directions if appropriate.

● **Alice Rozelle's Self-Diagnosis.** Hal hardly lifts a finger around the house. He comes home from work and just plops himself down in front of the TV. I come home from work, fix dinner, talk with the kids, serve dinner, clean up the kitchen, etc., etc., etc. I get really angry sometimes, especially when there's lots to do and I'm feeling particularly tired. Sometimes I lose my temper and scream at Hal to do something.

When I went through the Skill Questionnaire, I realized that I hadn't really been telling Hal what I'd like him to do. I was expecting him to do things because he wanted to. Well, he *doesn't* want to help. Who does, when someone else does it all? It seemed to me there's a chance that he would help, though, if I gave him clear instructions on what to do and *asked* him rather than yelled at him.

Skill Use: In thinking about the skill "Giving Instructions," I decided that I needed to figure out some specific jobs for Hal to do. That seemed to be the key to having him change his behavior. I decided that a good place to start was to ask him to do a chore on the way home from work. This way, I could discuss it calmly with him the night before. Later, after I practiced for a while, I could spontaneously give him instructions when something needed doing around the house at the moment. That would be more difficult to do without losing my temper, so I felt that I should do the easier one first. [1] On Monday, I knew we'd be needing milk and bread for Tuesday's dinner. [2] So, after dinner on Monday, I asked Hal to please pick them up on his way home from work the next day. [3] I told him which store had the kind of bread the kids liked. [4] At first, he was pretty surprised. I usually do all the shopping, as well as all the complaining about the shopping, and his reaction seemed to convey that he thought I never trusted his judgment. After the look of shock left his face, he said he would rather go to the store that evening, as the traffic would be lighter. [5] I smiled, said thanks, and he left. Wow, what results! Next week, I plan to ask Hal to help with the dinner cleanup. I think he may fall off his chair. While I'm at it, I'm also going to work on giving clearer instructions to the kids about doing chores around the house.

SKILL 7: Expressing Affection

Steps in expressing affection:

[1] Decide if you have warm, caring feelings about the other person.

[2] Decide whether the other person would like to know about your feelings.

[3] Decide how you might best express your feelings.

[4] Choose the right time and place to express your feelings.

[5] Express affection in a warm and caring manner.

● **Dave Becker's Self-Diagnosis.** It sounds funny, but I'll have to admit that after all these years of marriage, I'm still not affectionate with Carol. I mean, we get along okay; we talk, usually about household problems, kids, money, the usual. And our sex life is all right. . . . Maybe that's it. Things are "all right"; we "get along," but that . . . something, that extra closeness that we had when we were first married got lost somewhere. Carol tries to laugh it off . . . says I never was very romantic, and that a mother of two school-age children shouldn't expect romance. But we both know that isn't true. Come to think of it, I can't remember the last time I really told Carol that I loved her, and I sure can't think of times in the past few years that our sex life has been more than routine. Routine is a good word for our married life . . . regular, sensible, dull . . .

    Skill Use: I decided that I wanted and needed to break the routine. I do love Carol, but I sure as hell never express any affection toward her. Well, as a way of beginning I read through the steps for "Expressing Affection." To be honest, my first reaction was, "I can't do this. This is silly. You don't follow steps to express affection." But then I thought about it awhile, and realized that following the steps is just intended to get me started, to help me express the kinds of things that I've inhibited all these years. So, I went back and thought through the steps in detail. [1] I decided that I really wanted to begin being more open and affectionate with Carol, [2] and I knew that Carol, despite her comments like "he's not romantic," wanted to hear them. [3] Now, I know myself to some degree, and I know that, at this point at least, I couldn't just say "I love you" right out of the blue. No, I needed an "occasion." And the occasion had to be some break in the routine. [4] So, I called home from work yesterday and said to Carol, "Can you get a sitter to stay with the kids for a few hours? I made dinner reservations for us at the Tiffany Room." I thought she was going to collapse right there and then! But she got someone to look after the kids, dressed, and we drove to the restaurant right after I got home. She still seemed a bit wary as we sat down to the table. After all, "sensible Dave" never took her to the Tiffany Room, especially in the middle of the week! [5] We ordered cocktails, and, a little nervously, I'll admit, I said, "I wanted us to come here because I wanted you to know that I love you." There, I said it, and Carol was surprised! A tear sort of welled up in the corner of each eye and she leaned over the table and kissed me. I was a little embarrassed, but I liked it! I don't know if last night signals any major "turning point." I know that I feel good about it, and so does Carol. And I know that breaking the ice after all those years was difficult. But I also know that I'll have to keep working at it so that we don't slip right back into our dull, sensible routine.

SKILL 8: Expressing a Complaint

Steps in expressing a complaint:

[1] Define what the problem is, and who's responsible.

[2] Decide how the problem might be solved.

[3] Tell that person what the problem is and how it might be solved.

[4] Ask for a response.

[5] Show that you understand his or her feelings.

[6] Come to agreement on the steps to be taken by each of you.

● **Elaine Callahan's Self-Diagnosis.** It sounds funny, but I don't know how to complain! Well, that's not entirely true. If I buy vegetables at the store, for example, and they're not fresh enough, I'll return them. No, the problem for me is not in stores, and not at work either. I hold my own there. My problem is more with people I know well. I hate to hurt a friend's feelings, so I usually keep the problem to myself and wind up feeling angry and resentful. I've noticed lately that I may make a snide crack or two, and that does help me to feel better for the moment. But I know that sarcasm doesn't solve anything for me, and it's really not fair to the other person. Let me give you a recent example.

My friend Mary and I both work at full-time jobs. We try to get together for lunch every week or so. We make a date for noon, and she saunters in at 12:20. I've usually been sitting there for 20 minutes, not wanting to order without her, looking at my watch and worrying whether I'll get back to work for a 1 P.M. appointment. I wind up not enjoying my lunch or Mary's company. I'd really like to be able to complain to my friend when something is bothering me.

Skill Use: [1] So I spent some time thinking about what exactly the problem was. It boiled down to my wanting to relax and enjoy myself at lunch. The main reason I couldn't relax was Mary's lateness. [2] I knew that I would feel a lot better if I just asked her to be more considerate, and tell me what time she could really make it to the restaurant. This would help me to plan my schedule accordingly. [3] So last Friday, when she called me about having lunch, I explained the problem to her and I told her that I'd like her to make our appointment for a time when she could really get there. [4] Then asked her how she felt about it. She said she was aware that I had been somewhat edgy the last few times we had lunch, and that she would try to do better on the scheduling problem. [5] I told her I realized she was busy and that last-minute things sometimes came up at work, but I didn't like waiting for her and then having to rush. I told her that I liked having the time to enjoy our visit. [6] Well, we talked a while and we decided that she would work on getting there on time. We're also going to have lunch at a place closer to where I work, so that I wouldn't have to rush out quite as early. Our plan has, for the most part, worked out well. Sometimes we still have to eat and run, but I think I can tell her how I feel without jeopardizing our friendship.

SKILL 9: Persuading Others

Steps in persuading others:

[1] Decide on your position and what the other person's is likely to be.

[2] State your position clearly, completely, and in a way that is acceptable to the other person.

[3] State what you think the other person's position is.

[4] Restate your position, emphasizing why it is the better of the two.

[5] Suggest that the other person consider your position for a while before making a decision.

● **Steve Townsend's Self-Diagnosis.** I'm an engineer, and I do all right at my work. I've been with the same company four years now, which is not too bad, considering how tough it's getting to find and keep a job. Even though I've been here for four years, I've never gotten a bonus (our company has "incentive bonus awards" for "outstanding performance"). Most of the other engineers who have been here that long have gotten at least one bonus, sometimes two or more. I spoke with Eric, my best friend at work, who got his first bonus award last year. He said he went in to see Mr. Phillips, the manager, and sort of persuaded him to recommend him for the bonus. But that seems to be my problem—persuading people like Mr. Phillips to do what I want or to see things my way.

Skill Use: The first thing I decided to do was to set a be-havior-change goal for myself. The goal was to get a bonus at work by persuading Mr. Phillips to recommend me. To do it, I knew I was going to need help—after all, I had never really tried to persuade Mr. Phillips about anything before! So I talked it over with my wife, Sally. She's been urging me all along to "do more" at work, so she was more than happy to help me! We decided to really work on it—write out a behavior-change contract, rehearse, the whole bit! The behavior-change-contract idea was a little hard for me to get into. My feeling was that either you do it or you don't. But Sally persuaded me to try it, saying that it becomes more of a commitment if you write it down. So that's what I did, with Sally's help. [Steve's contract appears on page 76.]

The next part of my plan, the rehearsal, took a little doing. First, I sort of thought through the whole thing—what I wanted to say, how I would say it, what Mr. Phillips might say, and how I would respond. After I thought it through, I went through it again, this time out loud in front of the bedroom mirror. Later, I asked Sally to help out, and we went through it again—she played the part of Mr. Phillips. The second time we tried it, she even gave me a little static, just to see how I would handle it. Well, after all this rehearsal, I felt ready for the real thing. The next day, I made an appointment to see Mr. Phillips in his office later that after-noon. It went something like this: [1] First, I decided what my position would be: I had worked there four years, had gotten good supervisory ratings, and felt that I should be in line for a bonus incentive award this year. I figured that Mr. Phillips might say something like, "Let's give it another year, Steve." About a half an hour before the appointment I began to get nervous, and was tempted to drop the whole thing. "No," I told myself, "you've come this far. The worst that can happen is that he'll turn you down."

Well, I decided to keep the appointment, and after going into Mr. Phillips's office on schedule, and making a little small talk, I got right to it: [2] "Mr. Phillips, the reason I asked to see

BEHAVIOR-CHANGE CONTRACT

Behavior-Change Goal: TO PERSUADE MR. PHILLIPS TO NOMINATE ME, BY THE FIRST OF JUNE, FOR A BONUS.

Behavioral Steps to be Followed:

1. DECIDE ON MY POSITION AND WHAT HIS IS LIKELY TO BE.

2. STATE MY POSITION CLEARLY AND COMPLETELY.

3. TELL MR. PHILLIPS WHAT I THINK HIS POSITION IS.

4. RESTATE MY POSITION, TELLING HIM WHY I THINK IT IS BETTER THAN HIS.

5. SUGGEST TO MR. PHILLIPS THAT HE CONSIDER MY POSITION BEFORE DECIDING.

Reward: IF I MAKE A GOOD ATTEMPT (WHETHER I ACTUALLY GET THE BONUS OR NOT) SALLY AND I WILL HAVE A DINNER OUT.

Negative Consequences: IF I DON'T GO TO SEE MR. PHILLIPS BY JUNE 1ST, I'LL CLEAN OUT THE ENTIRE BASEMENT.

Bonus: IF I GET THE BONUS AT WORK, SALLY AND I WILL ALSO GIVE OURSELVES A BONUS: A 3-DAY-WEEKEND VACATION.

Record-Keeping: MARK TALLIES ON THE CALENDAR EACH TIME I PRACTICE.

Beginning Date: 5/12   Ending Date: 6/12

Signature: STEVE Townsend

you today was about the bonus–incentive awards. I know that nominations are due soon, and I sort of feel that I'm due for one. I've been here for just over four years, and my record has been good. [3] I've heard that sometimes you like people to hold off a while, but [4] I really think I deserve an award this year. [5] Could I check back with you in a couple of days to see what you've decided?" That's where I left it, but I didn't have to check back with him. He called me into his office early the next morning to tell me that the letter had just gone in—with my name on it.

SKILL 10: Expressing Anger

Steps in expressing anger:

[1] Pay attention to those body signals that help you know what you're feeling.

[2] Decide which outside events may have caused you to have these feelings.

[3] Decide if you're feeling angry about these events.

[4] Decide how you can best express these angry feelings.

[5] Express your angry feelings in a direct and honest manner.

● **Michelle Fine's Self-Diagnosis.** I have a lot of difficulty in expressing my angry feelings. When someone does or says something that makes me angry, I either walk away from the situation when I shouldn't or blow up before I realize what I'm doing. Then I inevitably feel bad, and I go overboard in trying to apologize. Yet, I'm aware that I seldom am able to say what I'm angry about at the time I'm experiencing the feeling, so I usually end up feeling frustrated. What I'd like to be able to do is to express my anger when I feel angry, and to let the other person know why I'm angry, rather than either shutting up or blowing up and then feeling guilty and apologetic. Yet I want to be able to do it in a way so that I don't have to attack the other person. I really must learn how to express my angry feelings more directly.

Skill Use: I thought about the behavioral steps for "Expressing Anger," and they made good sense to me. I certainly wasn't following the steps! After I read through the steps a couple of times, I thought about situations in which I've become angry recently—at the supermarket, with my husband, with the kids. I thought how I'd begin to feel tense and clench my jaw when these things happen. Then I imagined how I could have handled those situations differently had I followed the behavioral steps—what I would say, what the other person would say, and so on. I was beginning to feel a bit more comfortable using the behavioral steps, but I realized that I needed more practice. So I got out our handy little tape recorder, set it up in front of my mirror in the bedroom, and went through the conversations again. But this time I did it out loud, and watched myself in the mirror. Well, after the third conversation I was feeling a lot more comfortable with the skill. Then I played the tape and listened to myself—it's amazing what you learn about how you come across by listening to a tape recording! After listening to the tape and making mental notes of some of the things I might improve—tone of voice, loudness, etc., I felt more in command of the skill than I ever had.

My first real-life trial came last Saturday morning. My husband is a great tennis player, and last year he convinced me to take lessons so we could play doubles. I took the lessons and practiced when I could, but I still wasn't very good, although I sort of enjoyed it. Well, last Saturday, Allen walked into the kitchen while I was washing the dishes. He suggested that after I was through with the housework we play tennis. [1] As soon as he asked, I felt like screaming at him about what he could do with his tennis racket. I felt my body tense up and my heart start racing. [2] I thought to myself, "He wants me to play tennis and yet he hasn't done a thing all morning to help me in the house. The trash is sitting there waiting to be taken out. I've worked hard, I feel exhausted, and he expects me to be full of enough energy to go play tennis!" [3] I was angry and upset because I didn't appreciate watching him lounging around the house all morning while I worked. [4] Instead of blowing up, or of trying to hold in the resentment, I decided that I had better tell him directly about my feelings. [5] "Look," I said, "when you suggested we play tennis, I started feeling angry. You haven't done a thing around the house all morning, and now you want to go play tennis. You could do some of the chores also. I work all morning with no help, and I don't have the energy to go and enjoy myself."

Allen was shocked. I guess he had noticed that I was kind of gruff and angry most Saturdays, but I had never before told him why, at least not directly. We talked more about how I felt, and he said he really didn't mind doing some of the work. So we sat down and worked out a plan to divide the Saturday chores.

SKILL 11: Responding to a Compliment

Steps in responding to a compliment:

[1] Listen openly to the compliment.
[2] Tell the other person how the compliment makes you feel.
[3] Thank the other person in a warm and sincere manner.

● **Jennie Chapman's Self-Diagnosis.** Accepting compliments gracefully and comfortably has always been hard for me. If someone compliments my dress, I'll usually say something like, "This old rag?" If someone tells me I've done a good job, I get flustered and begin crediting others even when I really do deserve the praise. When this happens, I really feel silly. After all, why shouldn't I enjoy a compliment every once in a while?

Skill Use: The goal I set for myself was to feel more comfortable in accepting compliments and to respond more appropriately when I am complimented. For me, the hardest part was to recognize what I usually did that made me uncomfortable, and try to respond more appropriately by following the steps. I realized that changing habits takes practice, so I began to rehearse what I might say if someone complimented me. First, I thought through possible situations when I might receive compliments. Then I began practicing out loud. It's really surprising how just a "thank you" sounds if you're not used to saying it, even in practice.

Real-life "thank yous" are harder, at least for me, but I was beginning to say them, mainly at work. I have to admit that the first few times, I said "thank you" and followed it with some dumb thing like "so-and-so really did more work on it than I did." After a while, though, I began to say "thank you" and then shut my mouth.

Compliments from special people have always been the hardest of all to deal with, but in many ways they're the most important. So I set myself up to deal with a real test. I've been dating a fellow, Alex, whom I care for a lot, but I've always had special difficulties with compliments from him. To test my developing confidence, I bought a new dress to wear for our Saturday dinner date. The dress, by the way, was a reward for practicing my skill at work. I knew Alex would notice. When he arrived the first words out of his mouth were, "Wow, you look terrific in that outfit!" [1] Instead of immediately getting flustered, I listened to him. [2] Then I said, "That really makes me feel good, that you like my new dress. [3] Thank you." That was all—no "Oh, this old rag!" or "Do you really like it?" Just a simple "Thank you."

SKILL 12: Responding to the Feelings of Others (Empathy)

Steps to responding to the feelings of others:

[1] Observe the other person's words and actions.

[2] Decide what the other person might be feeling, and how strong the feelings are.

[3] Decide whether it would be helpful to let the other person know you understand his or her feelings.

[4] Tell the other person, in a warm and sincere manner, how you think he or she is feeling.

● **Cathy Schmidt's Self-Diagnosis.** A recent incident at work made me see how easy it is for me to ignore the feelings of people I care about. We were in the teacher's room and one of the teachers I often eat lunch with was angry with a student she had in class earlier. She was telling me how upset she felt. Instead of really getting involved, I simply shrugged my shoulders and sat there. Finally, she stopped talking to me and told the story to someone else who seemed to be more understanding.

Skill Use: I made up my mind that I needed to be more responsive to the feelings of my friends and colleagues and let them know that I can understand what they're feeling. I found that the best way for me to prepare for those situations was to play a little game while I was watching TV. I would watch an actor, and then try to think through how he or she was feeling. Usually, before too long, the actor would either confirm or disprove my guess. I also reviewed the steps for "Responding to the Feelings of Others," which got me thinking about empathy in a different way from the way I had in the past.

The last step says to tell the other person how you think he or she is feeling. I thought about a couple of recent instances at work, like the one I mentioned before, and I realized that typically, even when I understood what someone was feeling, I rarely let them know it. I went over the incident in my mind again and figured out some things I might have said. The day after I thought through all of this, I had another opportunity at school to put my practice to work. [1] I was on my way down the hall to drop off some things in the office. I heard one of the vice principals yelling at some students to move to class. When one of the students talked back to him, Mr. Perkins answered, "I don't want to hear any lip from you—just get to class!" He looked and sounded very stern.

[2] Mr. Perkins usually smiles and kids around with the students while getting them to move to class. Not this time. He was gruff, demanding, stiff, his face was red, and his fists were clenched. It looked as if the students had really gotten to him that morning. He was really angry. [3] When I got to the office and took care of the business I had there, I debated whether I

should say anything to him. Several things went through my head. First, I thought, "It was none of my business and he will cool down eventually without any interference from me. Better to leave things alone." Second, I thought, "If I say something, he'll get angry with me and tell me to mind my own business. Then I'll feel very bad. Yet if I do tell him that I understood his feelings, at least he'll know someone cared enough and maybe it would help. Should I risk getting verbally blasted?"

I decided to try to approach him. [4] Talk about approaching cautiously and treading lightly! I said, "Mr. Perkins, I just saw you a couple of minutes ago and you seemed very angry about something. That just isn't like you and I'd hate to see you like this all day. Is there anything I can do?" He replied angrily, "You'd be mad too if you found a $300 plate-glass window broken when you arrived at school." He went on for a while about students in general, and as he talked his anger lessened. I listened, and when he was finished, I told him that I didn't understand student vandalism either, and that it was a rough problem to have to deal with. In many ways, I felt helpless. After all, I couldn't do anything about the window. But Mr. Perkins looked calmer after we talked. It seemed to help him to get it off his chest.

SKILL 13: Following Instructions

Steps in following instructions:

[1] Listen carefully while the instructions are being given.

[2] Give your reactions to the instructions.

[3] Repeat the instructions to yourself.

[4] Imagine yourself following the instructions and then do it.

● **Frank Lazarro's Self-Diagnosis.** This winter I planned to take up skiing. I had never been on a pair of skis in the entire 37 years of my life. I wanted to learn, but I was a little pessimistic, since I often get frustrated learning new things. Instead of buying the equipment, I decided to rent it since I wasn't sure how much I would enjoy skiing. The Sports Center offered four free beginner's lessons with the rental, so I decided to take advantage of the chance.

I arrived two Fridays ago for my first lesson. Needless to say, I was scared to death. There were just two of us in the class; the other person was a 12-year-old boy who had all the agility and daring that I seemed to lack. Because of my fear I really couldn't concentrate on what the instructor was saying. I just wanted to get through the lesson without hurting myself. The instructor recommended that we practice at least once before the next lesson. Well, when I went over to practice by myself during the week, I found I couldn't remember how she had told us to negotiate a turn and I became very frustrated. I decided the next lesson would be different.

Skill Use: I reviewed the behavioral steps for following instructions, so that when I arrived at my next lesson, I felt better able to absorb what the instructor was saying. [1] In the beginning of the lesson she reviewed all the procedures, step by step, that we had done the week before. This time, I made sure that I listened very carefully to what she said. [2] When she finished explaining, I told her I didn't remember what she said about the turns last week, and her review of the instructions this week was like hearing it for the first time. I asked if I had it straight and I began repeating what she had said. She told me I was correct. Then she re-emphasized some important points. She then suggested that we take the lift to the top of the beginners' slope and try coming down, using the proper moves.

[3] While I was on the lift, I kept repeating the instructions to myself. [4] And when John (the 12-year-old) was going down the slope, I mentally saw myself going through all the things I should do: stand with my legs apart, knees flexed, my body forward so the shins of my legs were pressing against the front of my boots, all the weight on the balls of my feet. Once I started down I would push the skis into a wedge position; when I felt secure enough, I would make a small hop using my body weight equally, and, while in this hop, turn toward the downhill part of the slope.

When I was again secure, I would push out with my right foot using my heel, to finish the turn. I remember thinking, "It sure is a lot to remember."

Well, John made it down successfully and it was my turn. I took a couple of deep breaths and started down the slope at an angle. The funny thing about this whole experience was that although my head kept sending messages down to my legs and feet, they didn't exactly respond the way they should. I arrived at the bottom without falling, but I won't say I was ready for the Olympics that day. The instructor said it just takes practice to get my head and body working together, and who knows—I may just graduate from the beginners' to the intermediate slope!

SKILL 14: Responding to Persuasion

Steps in responding to persuasion:

[1] Listen openly to the other person's position.

[2] Consider the other person's possible reasons for that position.

[3] Ask the other person to explain anything you don't understand about what was said.

[4] Compare the other person's position with your own, identifying the pros and cons of each.

[5] Decide what to do, based on what will benefit you most in the long run.

● **Debby Freedman's Self-Diagnosis.** Beginning to socialize with men since my divorce has been kind of hard to adjust to. One of the main problems with my marriage was my feeling that I had to go along with what my husband wanted just because I was his wife. Now I'm single again—"my own woman"—and I find that I'm getting the same kind of pressure from the men I've been dating. On a few occasions, someone has asked me out and talked me into going someplace or doing something that I would have preferred not do. I find myself thinking, "If I don't go along with what he wants to do, he won't call me again." And I'm still not comfortable with the loneliness. It's a real conflict for me: Should I allow myself to be persuaded to do something I don't really want to, or should I sit here alone?

Skill Use: The more I thought about it, the more I became convinced that it didn't have to be an either/or situation, that is, either I get persuaded to do something I don't want to, or I sit home. That kind of thinking doesn't make sense. I knew it had to be possible to express my preference and still be liked. Being passive would just lead me into another relationship like the one I had with my husband. It was sort of reassuring to talk to Margo, a woman who works with me—she went through the same thing about a year ago. She encouraged me to make up my own mind about what I wanted to do. Margo's advice helped, but I also needed more practice in responding to people's attempts to persuade me to do things that I might not want to do. So I thought through recent situations in which I could have used the steps for responding to persuasion. I also discussed them with Margo and she gave me some "What ifs": "What if Bill (a fellow I've dated a few times) asks you . . . ?" "What if . . . ?"

Last week something came up where I could put my practice to the test. [1] Bill invited me to a party on Saturday night given by some people at his office. I told him I'd like to think about it. I don't know any of those people, and in the past when I've been taken to someone's office party, I've felt really awkward —everyone there seems content to "talk shop," and I don't enjoy that at all. [2] I just didn't know whether Bill mainly wanted to be with me, or whether he mainly wanted to go to the party and needed someone to take along. [3] I'll have to admit that it took more courage than I thought I had, but when Bill called me back, I said to him, "I'd really like to go out with you, Bill, but I've really soured on office parties. Can you tell me what you expect this one to be like?" [4] I think my reply surprised him. He sputtered a little and then said, "Well, to be honest, I guess it will be pretty dull. I'd like you to come along, because to tell the truth, I don't much enjoy those parties either."

I thought about what he said; I appreciated his honesty; but I still didn't want to go to the party. [5] "Look, Bill," I said, "I can understand your feeling that you ought to go to the party. But I don't think I'd really enjoy it. Why don't I take a rain check."

Bill's reply pleasantly surprised me: "Let me try to make some excuse at work tomorrow, and then the two of us can have a quiet dinner somewhere."

"I'd like that," I said, and I meant it. I hung up the telephone and congratulated myself on following through with what I had set out to do.

SKILL 15: Responding to Failure

Steps in responding to failure:

[1] Decide if you have failed.

[2] Think about both the personal reasons and the circumstances that have caused you to fail.

[3] Decide how you might do things differently if you tried again.

[4] Decide if you want to try again.

[5] If it is appropriate, try again, using your revised approach.

● **Hal Week's Self-Diagnosis.** The fellows at work have been trying to cheer me up about "the single life" since my divorce from my wife about six months ago. I'm sure they mean well when they talk about all the women in my life. But to tell the truth, dating after all those years of marriage terrifies me. And it's not just the dating, it's asking a woman out! "What if she turns me down?" is what I keep saying to myself. I've only had about two real dates since the divorce, and those came about only because someone fixed me up. I did make a couple of attempts to ask women for dates, but I got turned down. Sue at the office said she had a boyfriend, and the other one I asked said she was busy that night. I understood what they said, but even so, I felt as if I had failed! Well, I decided that I had to start doing things differently because I really did want to begin dating again.

Skill Use: I read through the behavioral steps for "Responding to Failure" and decided to apply them to my dating situation. I thought through my previous attempts at asking women out and figured out how I might have handled them differently had I applied the steps. "Next time, things will be different," I told myself.

Well, my chance to try it out came last week. There was a concert scheduled for Saturday and I really wanted to go. Not only that, I really wanted to take a date to the concert. Since the seats would probably go quickly, I bought two good ones last Monday. Then I thought about whom I could ask. My first thought was Mary, a girl who works in the same building as I do. She always smiles and says "hello" when I see her in the elevator, but I've never seen her outside of work. Well, I got her telephone number from personnel, and I called her up last Monday night. We talked for a while and she was pleasant enough, but when I asked her out she said, "I'd really love to, Steve, but I have other plans."

[1] My first thought was, "Shot down again. What's the use? I'll just turn in the extra ticket at the box office." But I had promised myself that I wouldn't give up. [2] I thought about why she had refused. Maybe she just didn't want to go out with me. Maybe she has a regular boyfriend. Maybe she really did have other plans. I really don't know anything about Mary. [3] I thought about whom else I might ask out, and about how I might do it differently. I remembered Joan, the woman I met at the open house at the Turners' last month. Instead of just calling her up out of the blue, I decided to find out what I could about Joan and whether she was dating anybody. I called Frannie Turner, who turned out to be a big help. She told me that Joan wasn't dating anyone steadily, and she encouraged me to give it a try. [4] Well, I decided to try again. [5] I called up Joan, who said she did remember me (I think Frannie might have tipped her off). We talked for quite a while over the phone. Then I invited

her to the concert. She said she would love to go; she had seen the announcement in the paper and had wanted to hear the group.

Well, we went out last night and had a really good time. I kind of like this new approach of getting some information about a woman's situation before asking her for a date. I realize that even with that, I will still get turned down if she's not interested, but I think the chances of that are much less.

SKILL 16: Responding to Contradictory Messages

Steps in responding to contradictory messages:

[1] Pay attention to those body signals that help you know you are feeling trapped or confused.

[2] Observe the other person's words and actions that may have caused you to have these feelings.

[3] Decide whether that person's words and actions are contradictory.

[4] Decide whether it would be useful to point out the contradiction.

[5] Ask the other person to explain the contradiction.

● **Stan Russo's Self-Diagnosis.** You know the feeling you get when you like someone and want to get to know her better, and you can't figure out what she feels—and pretty soon you don't know whether you're coming or going? Let me tell you about what's been going on with this girl, Susan. We would get to talking in the cafeteria or the elevator, and we'd really be having a good time. Then I'd ask her if we could get together some time, and she'd say she'd like to very much and why don't I give her a call. So I would call her up, and she'd say how glad she was that I called and all, but she was busy with this or that. Then we'd run into each other in the street, really hit it off, and she'd say again how much she'd like to get together, and I'd call up and she'd be busy again with something. Well, this was going on for, I don't know, a few weeks. And all the time I'm figuring there must be something wrong with me, that she doesn't really like me and all. Then it occurred to me that she's really been giving me contradictory messages and I'm not dealing with them very well.

Skill Use: The main problem I was having in trying to deal with double messages was to realize what the other person was doing at the time it happened. I figured the best way I could do that was to think through times when it happened in the past—think about how I could have applied the steps, and about how I could have handled those situations differently. I also thought about situations that might come up in the near future, particularly with Susan. She really has a knack for saying opposite things at the same time. After I had done all that, I didn't have to wait long for a real-life test. I ran into her the very next week and I'll be damned if it didn't start happening again. I really felt attracted to her, and I thought that she seemed to like me. So we got to talking, and she began telling me, "We really have to get together."

[1] Right away, I got this really tense feeling, as if my whole body were tightening up. I began thinking to myself, "What's going on here? I'm all tense and confused!" [2] I looked at her and I could see that she was uncomfortable too—I could almost hear her saying, "We really have to get together"—but kind of blushing and nervous, and not looking at me. [3] So I began thinking, "Something's wrong here; she says she wants to get together, but she's saying it like she doesn't mean it or something—she's not even looking at me." [4] I decided that this was getting ridiculous—I had to find out what was going on. What was she doing—playing games? [5] So I said, "Susan . . . you know you're always saying how we have to get together, and to call you up and all . . . and when I do you're always busy, or you act like you're not interested. Like right now, you say let's get together, but you sound like maybe you don't mean it. Like you were looking away when you said it. You've really got me confused here."

She got real embarrassed, but then we talked about it, and she told me she really would like to get to know me better, but she was kind of scared of getting close, of getting involved. I think both of us felt better after that, as if just talking about it had brought us closer together. I guess I was reading the situation accurately all along. She was saying yes and no at the same time.

SKILL 17: Responding to a Complaint

Steps in responding to a complaint:

[1] Listen openly to the complaint.

[2] Ask the person to explain anything you don't understand.

[3] Show that you understand the other person's thoughts and feelings.

[4] Tell the other person your thoughts and feelings, accepting responsibility if appropriate.

[5] Summarize the steps to be taken by each of you.

● **Nancy Gauthier's Self-Diagnosis.** I'm the type of person who puts as much as she can into whatever she does. I devote a lot of time and effort to my work and usually get a lot of satisfaction from a job well done. Recently I've become aware that I get very upset whenever someone criticizes my work. I take it very personally, and it makes me feel like I'm not very worthwhile. At first I'm inclined to retreat. Then I begin to dislike the person who complains, and then I go through a lot of "I should have saids." In fact, it happened last week.

I was very busy with my work and inadvertently walked into my boss's office when he was with a client. Later, he complained to me that I had interrupted a *very* important meeting. Well, I muttered and sputtered an awkward apology, I even thought about quitting, and then I started with my usual "I should have saids." I realize that I sometimes do things that people will complain about (who doesn't?), but I'd like to be able to handle their complaints better.

Skill Use: I decided that this was a problem area that I could use some help with. So I asked Steve, my husband, if he would help out. (I don't have any trouble handling the occasional complaint that Steve has.) Anyway, I sort of decided how I should respond to complaints by following the behavioral steps, and then I went over likely situations in my imagination. At that point, I asked Steve if he would take the role of my boss, the person whose complaints I have a lot of trouble handling. I described what happened when I interrupted the boss's meeting, and we rehearsed how I might have acted differently, following the behavioral steps. Here's how it went:

Steve (Boss): [1] "Nancy, I'm very disappointed, and a bit annoyed about your walking into my office this morning when I was with a client. It was a very important meeting."

Nancy: [2] "Yes, I know. Is there some way I can know for sure if someone is in there with you? Your door is always closed."

Boss: "I keep a list of my appointments on my desk calendar. Maybe you should check it first thing each morning."

Nancy: [3] "I understand that it was uncomfortable for you when I walked in when your client was there. [4] However, I hope you realize that I didn't know you had an appointment at that time. I'll be more careful from now on. [5] If you'll keep the appointment schedule on your desk calendar, then I'll be sure to check it every morning."

Boss: "I will. Thank you; I'd appreciate your checking it."

Well, after this rehearsal with Steve (we actually went through it a couple of times), I felt pretty comfortable in applying the steps for responding to a complaint. I felt ready to deal with the next complaint from my boss at work.

SKILL 18: Concentrating on a Task

Steps in concentrating on a task:

[1] Set a realistic goal.

[2] Decide on a reasonable time schedule.

[3] Gather the materials you need.

[4] Arrange your surroundings to minimize distraction.

[5] Judge whether your preparation is complete and begin the task.

● **Ken Burns's Self-Diagnosis.** I'm a guy you might call "easily distracted." It's not true all the time, however. I notice that if I'm really interested in doing something, I get it done. It's the chores and projects that I don't particularly care about that I avoid, interrupt, postpone, and generally can't concentrate on. Let me give you an example. We're going to be selling our house because I'm getting transferred to another city in a couple of months. We talked to a real estate agent who told us that we could probably sell it for more money if I got a few of the rooms painted. And we'll sure need the extra money if we're going to be able to buy a nice house when we move. Well, I've been putting it off and putting it off and finally came to the conclusion that I needed some help in concentrating on painting the house.

   Skill Use: I realized that I needed to apply the steps for "Concentrating on a Task" to the job at hand—painting the living room, dining room, downstairs hall, and small bedroom. So, I decided to think through the steps, one at a time, before starting to use them. My thinking went something like this: [1] First, I need to set a realistic goal. "Finish the painting in four weeks" sounded realistic to me. [2] I will work on one area at a time, and allow one weekend for each. No, if I really work at it, I might be able to finish each room in one day. Okay, I'll allow four Saturdays to do the job, with time left on the Sundays if I need to do some finishing up. [3] Gather materials—now, this is where I usually fall down. I'm always out of something, and then I have to stop what I'm doing and go to the store. Not this time. I will get the dimensions of the rooms and take them to the paint store tonight. The salesman and I will figure out how much paint I need. I'll also get a couple of new brushes and some dropcloths. I already have a good painting ladder. Everything will then be ready to go. [4] Minimize distractions—they also do me in. The kids want me to drive them somewhere, my wife wants to go shopping, you name it. This time will be different. I'll discuss it with Cindy and the kids tonight at dinner. They're all going someplace together tomorrow, to the new shopping mall, I think, so I'll be here alone. That will give me a good start. [5] I really think that will complete the preparations. You know, somehow the job feels more manageable now that I have it broken down into smaller pieces. I don't think it will be too difficult to concentrate, using the plan I've mapped out.

SKILL 19: Preparing for a Stressful Conversation

Steps in preparing for a stressful conversation:

[1] Imagine yourself in the stressful situation.

[2] Think about how you will feel and why you will feel that way.

[3] Imagine the other person in the stressful situation. Think about how that person will feel and why he or she will feel that way.

[4] Imagine yourself telling the other person what you want to say.

[5] Imagine the response that that will elicit.

[6] Repeat the above steps using as many approaches as you can think of.

[7] Choose the best approach.

● **Ed Riley's Self-Diagnosis.** The last time I went for a job interview, I thought I'd just be myself. You know, just go in there, no preparation, be completely spontaneous. I'd say what I felt, and it'd work out in the end. So I went for this interview, and, well, it started out all right. But then the employer started asking me some questions that I just didn't expect, like why I left my last job, did I have trouble getting along with my last employer, why did I want to work for this company, and so on. I don't know, all those questions just knocked me off balance. I felt like I was being put on the spot, and I wasn't prepared to deal with his questions. As it turned out, I didn't get the job.

Skill Use: Well, that was the end of my "spontaneous" approach. I was going to be sure I was well prepared for my next interview by going through the necessary steps. I decided to rehearse the day before the interview. [1] I spent some time imagining my walking into the office to talk to the interviewer. [2] I knew I'd be nervous by the very nature of the situation. The focus would be on me, and I'd want to make a good impression, say the right things, appear interested, alert. Knowing how I have a tendency to get nervous in these situations might make the interview more difficult than usual. [3] I had to assume that the interviewer wouldn't go out of his way to make me feel comfortable. I mean if I had to pick an employee I'd want to make sure I was getting the right person for the job and I'd be listening very carefully to everything he had to say. I'd want to get all the facts, all the credentials. [4] So this time, I was going to make a real effort to present all my strong points: my experience, my recommendations, how much I enjoyed the type of work, and why I wanted to work for this company.

I tried to remember any other questions I was asked at my last interview so that this time I could have it work to my advantage. [5] Then I tried to imagine how the interviewer would respond and any tricky questions he might ask—like if I did well at my last job, why did I leave it; did I get along with my last employer, etc. [6] I'd tell him that I left my last job because of the distance from my home—it was too far and therefore too difficult to get to. Also, I much preferred to sell furniture than clothing since my career interest and most of my experience were in that area.

I also figured that I'd better be prepared for the unusual hours, like working evenings and on Saturday, and to say that that was fine with me. [7] I decided the best approach was to emphasize all my strong points, be ready to explain anything about my experience or record that might be taken the wrong way, and to express enthusiasm about this particular job and company. After rehearsing it all in my mind, I felt more calm about the actual interview and more confident about my chances of getting the job.

SKILL 20: Making Decisions

Steps in making decisions:

[1] Gather accurate information about the topic.

[2] Evaluate the information in light of your goal.

[3] Make a decision that is in your best interest.

● **Curt Jackson's Self-Diagnosis.** I never seem to be able to come to a decision when I'm shopping—especially when I'm about to buy something I really want, and it costs a lot. Last week I wanted to buy a camera. I went into this store and started looking around. There were several cameras I was interested in. I tried asking the salesman, but he gave me this line on how they're all good and it depends on what I want. I guess I never stopped to think about what I wanted, what kind of camera, how much I was willing to pay, things like that. I should've asked the salesman for more information or asked for another salesman. I just didn't know what I wanted, and I obviously needed more information. I must have been in there more than an hour before I just left the damned place. I've got to be able to make better decisions about what to buy.

Skill Use: Well, I still wanted a camera, and I finally bought one. I was able to do it because I decided to apply the behavioral steps to my decision about which camera to buy. [1] First, I read up a little about different kinds of cameras, advantages and disadvantages of each, the price ranges, and all the special features. I spoke to my friend Bob. He does a lot of photography, and gave me some helpful advice. Then I went to the store. This time I had a list of questions prepared, and I asked the salesman in the store to give me specific information about some of their cameras.

[2] I figured I needed to mull over what to do, so I left the store and went for a walk to help me think. I've gotten really interested in photography, and I plan to spend a lot of my free time with it, so I figured I should buy myself a really decent camera, not a piece of garbage. But I still didn't need anything too fancy; after all, I wasn't a professional. I certainly didn't need any of those cameras the salesman showed me with all those extras and ultra-high-powered lenses. But it didn't make sense to buy some of the cheap stuff he showed me either. Finally, I settled on a couple of cameras I liked and could afford. [3] I went back into the store and found the salesman again. I think the salesman really knew his business and, remembering a few things that Bob had told me and that I had read, I decided on one without too much difficulty. I'm really pleased with myself for buying that camera. And it wasn't so bad shopping around this time. I kind of enjoyed it.

SKILL 21: Determining Responsibility

Steps in determining responsibility:

[1] Decide what the problem is.

[2] Consider possible causes of the problem.

[3] Decide which are the most likely causes of the problem.

[4] Take actions to test out which are the actual causes of the problem.

● **Pete Konski's Self-Diagnosis.** I'm the kind of person who takes his responsibilities seriously. If I take on a job, I always make sure it's done right. If I borrow something and promise to return it by a certain date, it's always returned right on time. Everyone says I'm very conscientious, sometimes *too* conscientious! For example, if something goes wrong at work, like last week when the duplicating machine broke down and we couldn't get the report out exactly on time, I felt as if it were my fault. Well, if I had stopped to think about it, I would have realized that it wasn't my fault at all; the machine just broke, and we did the best we could under the circumstances. But my first impulse was to blame myself, and to start apologizing all over the place. I've got to learn how to determine responsibility more accurately.

Skill Use: Betty, my wife, has been my biggest help with the problem. She was reading over the behavioral steps for "Determining Responsibility" and pointed out to me that they were exactly what I was not doing. We talked about different situations that have come up recently when I've taken blame on myself when it wasn't justified—at work, around the house, at the lodge. We figured out how I could have handled the situations differently if I'd followed the behavioral steps. I resolved, with Betty's help, to deal with the next situation differently by following those steps.

I didn't have long to wait. I had borrowed my next-door neighbor's lawn mower yesterday, and promised to return it today. Well, when I went out this morning, [1] I discovered that the mower wouldn't start. [2] My first thought was that I had broken it, and I was ready to go have it fixed. But I thought about it and decided, with Betty's help, to consider what might be causing it not to start. I checked the gas, the oil, the cable, everything I thought might be wrong. [3] I narrowed the likely causes of the problem down to the spark plug and the cable that connects to it. [4] By this time, I was pretty sure that I hadn't caused the trouble with the mower, so I decided to tell Sid, my neighbor, about the problem and see what he thought.

I guess I was still a little afraid that Sid would blame me, but, to my surprise, he told me he had been having the same problem for months, and that it certainly wasn't my fault. Together we checked out the spark plug and the cable. It turned out to be a worn-out plug. We drove to the store together, and Sid bought the part he needed. I was almost ready to offer to pay for it, but I remembered that I was not responsible for the problem with the mower. As things turned out, Sid thanked me for my help and told me I could use the mower any time I needed it.

SKILL 22: Self-Control

Steps to self-control:

[1] Pay attention to those body signals that help you know you're about to lose control of yourself.

[2] Decide which outside events may have caused you to feel frustrated.

[3] Consider ways in which you might control yourself.

[4] Choose the most effective way of controlling yourself and do it.

● **Brian Honig's Self-Diagnosis.** Sometimes things just start getting out of hand, and before I know it I'm blowing my stack. I've noticed it a lot recently, particularly with my son, Johnny. At work, and even with my wife, Sandy, I'm able to control my temper pretty well. But with kids, with Johnny, well . . . ! For example, one night about a week or two ago, I came home from work really bushed, and a little tense (there's some reorganizing going on at work, and I'm in the middle of it). And you know kids. There was Johnny, running around, screaming, playing cowboys. I was getting a terrible headache, so I yelled, "Dammit, stop it." But I guess he was too wrapped up in his playing. Maybe he didn't hear me. But I kept getting madder and madder—all that noise! Finally, I grabbed him by the arm and really bawled him out: "Look, I told you to stop it! You listen to me when I tell you something!" I guess I scared him. He ran into his room, crying.

I realized afterward that I had really lost control of myself. How was he supposed to know that I had a headache? I felt upset and ashamed for having yelled at him like that. But what that episode did was to make me aware that I had to do something about my ability to control myself better.

Skill Use: I read through the steps for self-control, and I really thought about them, especially steps 1 and 2. I realized that I usually don't pay much attention to how I'm feeling at the time I get upset, it just seems to happen. But when I thought about the incident with Johnny, I could have figured it out. The headache was my main body signal, and I sure as hell knew what was going on that could have caused it! Figuring out the best ways of controlling myself wasn't as difficult. I thought about what worked for me at the office. I usually closed my door and spent a few minutes by myself. Or sometimes, I counted to ten and actually said things like "calm down" to myself. Now, what I needed to practice was tuning into body signals and figuring out what caused the upset. So, for the next week, every time I was feeling a little tense or frustrated, I made a concerted effort to use those two steps.

I was feeling a little better about being able to control myself, but I hadn't really had to deal with a situation involving Johnny lately. That is, one hadn't come up until last night. It began as almost an exact repeat of the last one. I came home from work tired, a little tense, preoccupied and wanting to be left alone. Then Johnny burst into the living room; this time he was a spaceman. [1] As I was sitting there trying to read the paper, I could feel myself getting more and more worked up. My teeth were clenched and my head began throbbing. [2] So I thought to myself, "It's that kid again, and all that goddamn noise!" [3] Then I thought to myself, "Okay, hold it! Don't start screaming at him—that only makes it worse. Maybe I should just leave the room—go outside or something. No, that's ridiculous; I want to sit here in the living room. Maybe I should just try to ignore the noise. No, I can't do that. Look, why don't I just tell Johnny to go play outside so that I can sit here quietly and read the paper. No sense getting all angry and excited.

[4] "Johnny, hey, Johnny. Come here a second. Why don't you go play outside a while. I'm kind of tired from work and I've got a headache, so I'd like to sit here and read the paper for a few minutes." And that was all there was to it. No fuss, no upset. He zipped right outside, and I calmed down in a matter of moments. And, most important for me, I got the feeling that I really controlled myself, and that's a good feeling to have!

SKILL 23: Negotiating

Steps in negotiating:

[1] State your position.
[2] State your understanding of the other person's position.
[3] Ask if the other person agrees with your statement of his or position.
[4] Listen openly to his or her response.
[5] Propose a compromise.

● **Richard Rose's Self-Diagnosis.** I've been feeling like Dr. Jekyll and Mr. Hyde for about the past year. I've always thought of myself as kind of an easy-going, flexible, let-people-do-what-they-want sort of a person. Beginning about a year ago, somehow my tolerance just wasn't there anymore. Whenever my wife and I had a discussion about anything where there was even a hint of disagreement, I found myself exploding at her and insisting that I have things my way. Later, I'd feel embarrassed about my tantrum, and go back and apologize and tell her to do things the way she wanted. Then I'd go off and sulk some more about how I could never get my own way around the house. Lately, I've made an effort to change things. Somehow, though, the change hasn't really helped how I've been feeling. I decided a few months ago *not* to raise my voice any more, even when I completely disagreed with what my wife was saying. Instead, I'd take a "yes, dear" attitude to whatever she said. The net result of my new stance was that I was walking around feeling unimportant and useless in the house. I felt resentful about winding up doing a bunch of things I didn't want to do, and I knew that the resentment showed, even though I did my best to hide it.

At work, the situation wasn't much different. Although I never had a full-blown temper tantrum at work, it was all I could do to keep from blowing my top. I found myself saying nothing at meetings when something important came up for discussion. Then, about an hour later, I'd start feeling angry and resentful because my point of view was never considered in making the final policy deicison. Basically, I knew that no one could consider my point of view when I hadn't opened my mouth, but I was afraid that if I opened my mouth I wouldn't be able to shut it again.

The idea of negotiation never even occurred to me until I took the Skill Questionnaire. Looking at the definition of "Negotiating," I read: "Arriving at a plan that satisfies both you and another person who has taken a different position." All of a sudden, it seemed so obvious. Compromise. That was what I needed to learn how to do. At home, it didn't have to be either Joan's way *or* my way. I could be her way today, and my way tomorrow. Or, it could be a little of her way and a little of my way. The situation wasn't as black and white as I had made it out to be.

Going through the behavioral steps for "Negotiating," I decided on a final goal of learning how to negotiate, or compromise on matters of disagreement at home and at work. I wanted to learn how to do this without blowing up, and without walking away feeling resentful. I was sick and tired of my Jekyll–Hyde personality.

Skill Use: The first step I decided to take in preparing to change my behavior was to do some record keeping. I needed to look at when and where I was having a problem so that I could tackle the situation in a logical way, working on the easier situations before going on to the tougher ones. So I decided to jot down in my pocket calendar each time I had a disagreement with someone that might possibly lead to compromise or negotiation. I did this for a week.

At the end of the week, I found that three times with my wife, and twice at work (once with my boss and once with a co-worker), I probably could have reached a compromise solution to a problem. As usual, at least lately, my response to these situations was a great big nothing. I didn't even bother to state my position on any of the matters we disagreed on, let alone try to negotiate a solution.

Mulling over the results of my record keeping, I decided to take on the problem at home before I worked on things at the office. I made this decision because I knew I needed help in changing my behavior and I knew Joan could help. She's been so ticked off at me lately about being an "absentee husband" that I knew she would support me in the changes I was trying to make. After all, there would be some rewards in it for her, too, if I got more involved in the decision-making around the house.

So, before doing anything else, I sat down with her and talked about what I wanted to do. I showed her the behavioral steps for "Negotiating" and let her know that I was going to try to get more involved in deciding things at home. I asked her if she would help by listening to me when I tried my new skill and give me some feedback about how I had done. I told her that once I got good at it, I'd try it out at work with Mr. Adamson (my boss) when it came to the issue of my department budget. Budget figures were due for discussion in about a month, and I thought that that would give me enough time to practice things at home.

Joan was delighted. She told me she'd do anything she could to help me. She said she knew I'd been sulking and irritable lately, and that she was glad that I had pinpointed the problem. One thing she brought up was that negotiation took two people following the steps, not just one. She said she would make an effort to follow the steps for negotiation also.

After I talked to her, I sat down to plan my next move. I decided to go the whole way and write a contract with myself. Then I wouldn't back down on my goals. I knew that Joan had been trying to get me involved in picking out some new carpeting for the living room. I had sidestepped the issue, because we can never seem to agree on furnishings for the house. She likes all of these bright colors, and I tend toward darker, more conservative things. I had been avoiding talking about the problem, and had let her do the shopping herself. I knew that if the carpet just arrived, without my being involved in the selection, I'd have to live with something like a shocking-pink floor for the next twenty years. It was certainly a good first topic for negotiation. So I chose that to write my contract about. [Richard's contract appears on page 104.]

The next evening, after dinner, Joan and I took our coffee into the living room, as usual. I told her that I'd like to talk about the carpeting, and that I was interested in negotiating with her about what kind to buy. I thought she was going to fall out of her chair. She had stopped talking about the carpeting weeks before, since she was getting no response from me. [1] I told her that I like carpeting that kind of blends into the background. Maybe a mustard color would be nice. [2] I said I knew she preferred brighter colors. [3] I asked her if that was right. She said yes, it was, and she felt that a bright-yellow carpet would be sunny and cheerful. [4] I listened while she talked, trying to understand her point of view. [5] I suggested that we go to the carpet store together, and maybe pick out something midway between mustard and bright yellow. Then we'd have something not too drab for her, but not a rug that would bowl me over very time I came into the room. We decided that we would go shopping the next night.

Well, Joan and I went to the carpet place the next day, and found something we both could live with. As I had promised myself, I took her out to dinner that Friday. I felt like I had made the first important move toward more involvement at home, and it felt good. Joan was certainly happy about it! She gave me good feedback on my negotiation skills and said that she was pleased

BEHAVIOR-CHANGE CONTRACT

Behavior-Change Goal: After supper tomorrow, negotiate calmly with Joan about the living-room carpet.

Behavioral Steps to be Followed:

1. State my position.
2. State to Joan what I think her position is.
3. Ask Joan if I am correct about what her position is.
4. Listen openly to her response.
5. Propose a Compromise.

_____

_____

Reward: Go out for dinner Friday if we have a discussion and come to a reasonable compromise.

Negative Consequences: If I blow up or back down, I'll volunteer to do dishes for the next week.

Bonus: If I negotiate successfully at work and at home I'll buy myself a new fishing rod.

Record-Keeping: Notes in my pocket calendar.

Beginning Date: Mar. 26. _____ Ending Date: June 1.

Signature: Richard Rose.

that she wouldn't have to make all of the decisions at home by herself any more.

After about a month of negotiating at home, successfully for the most part (I continued to keep track in my pocket calendar), I felt that I was ready to tackle Mr. Adamson at work. I talked it over with Joan, and she agreed that I hadn't been hotheaded or "absentee" for quite a while. And she pointed out that we'd worked out problems several times in the last couple of weeks. She said she felt I was ready to deal with Mr. Adamson.

I decided on a different strategy for tackling the work problem from the one I had used at home. I knew what the issue would be at work—the budget for my section—and I felt that I had to do some rehearsing. Unlike at home, where Joan and I could talk about how I'd done, I needed to do my negotiating at work the right way the first time through. Mr. Adamson is a rather brusque man. He assumes that he knows what's best for everybody in the office. For the last two years, my section has received budget cuts to the point where we're operating on a shoestring. Yet Frank Tucci, who heads the bookkeeping section, has gotten as much money as he needs each year to keep his department operating well. I know that Frank has gone in and talked to Mr. Adamson about his budget needs. But I've just accepted what Mr. Adamson has handed out. I knew it would be hard to talk with him, particularly because I feel kind of resentful about how my department had been treated.

The first step was to rehearse in my imagination. I thought about walking into Mr. Adamson's office and telling him that we needed to talk about my department's budget. [1] I would tell him that the current budget just wasn't adequate for the department to operate effectively. I'd give him some examples of how the budget cuts had been inefficient. [2] Then I'd tell him that I knew he was under pressure to keep operating costs as low as possible, and he probably hadn't considered raising our department's budget request. [3] Next I'd ask him if I understood his position correctly. [4] I'd listen while he talked about the company's financial crunch, and try to understand his point of view. [5] Then I'd ask him if he could consider some compromise solution; perhaps he could juggle some funds that have been earmarked for less-necessary items than the ones I mentioned. I'd let him know quite clearly that I understood that *all* of my needs couldn't be met, and that I didn't expect him to bankrupt other departments for my sake.

After imagining the scene a few times, I decided to rehearse in front of the mirror. I talked to the mirror, and I must admit that even though I was alone, I got a little tense about getting the words out. When I had done it calmly a few times, I asked Joan if she'd help me rehearse. She played Mr. Adamson, and I tried to negotiate with her. I had to remind her a few times to act like Mr. Adamson, and not to be "understanding Joan." She finally got the hang of what behavioral rehearsal was about, and we got into a good session of rehearsing. Then she gave me some good feedback about how I had done. She told me that my voice sometimes sounded whining, and that probably Mr. Adamson would not react positively to that. I tried it again, and managed to say what I wanted in a firm, more self-confident voice. I decided that I was finished with the rehearsal stage when I felt absolutely calm going through the rehearsal with Joan, even when she gave me a bit of a hard time.

Well, the next step was the real thing. I sat down with myself that night and decided to tackle the problem the next day. I knew I should build in some rewards for "good behavior," so I spent some time thinking about what I could do for myself if I got through the meeting with Mr. Adamson with flying colors. I knew that one very important reward would be his respect. Another would be the reward of the increased budget (I hoped). But I thought I should do something extra for myself as a bonus if things went just as I planned, and if I didn't mess up at all. Joan and I had been talking about going on a ski weekend for ages, and it seemed like a good time to make those plans concrete—if I did a good job negotiating.

Things turned out the way I hoped they would. Mr. Adamson agreed to consider *some* of my budget requests, and I agreed to give up some others. Joan and I are leaving for our ski weekend in exactly nine days.

Next job? To hang onto what I've learned. I can't let myself slide back into old habits. It's much better not to feel so resentful all the time.

SKILL 24: Assertiveness

Steps in assertiveness:

[1] Pay attention to those body signals that help you know that you're dissatisfied and would like to stand up for yourself.

[2] Decide which outside events may have caused you to feel dissatisfied.

[3] Consider ways you might stand up for yourself.

[4] Take your stand in a direct and reasonable manner.

● **Jean Arnold's Self-Diagnosis.** "Good old reliable Jean." You know, someone actually called me that just last week. Another "good cause," and they needed a neighborhood volunteer. I'm the person who "volunteers" to collect for every charity, who's always in charge of the clean-up committee at the annual church bazaar, who has been room mother at school for as long as I can remember, who will sit with neighbors' children so they can run a few errands, who will lend my car because someone else's is in the shop . . . the list is endless. Many times I don't mind helping out and doing favors. The charities I work for are those in which I really believe. But sometimes—a lot of the time—I can't seem to say no.

I used to tell myself, "They'd do it for you if you needed a favor" or "someone's got to do it," but I don't say those things as much anymore. More often than not, I'm finding myself feeling uptight and resentful when someone asks me for a favor. But, uptight or not, I still do it, and I get angry with myself for doing things I don't really want to. So, I decided it was time to try to do something about it and begin asserting myself when I want to.

Skill Use: The first thing I did was to read through the steps for "Assertiveness." It was certainly clear to me that I wasn't following the steps. In particular, I discovered that the thing I wasn't doing was tuning into my body signals and I wasn't deciding whether I wanted to go along with the requests everyone made. One important fact I read about was that habits don't change over night. You have to recognize each situation in which you use a bad habit, and you have to work at changing each time. Before doing any changing, I felt it would be useful for me to keep track of situations in which I didn't assert myself but could have. I decided to do that for two weeks.

I'm a list-maker and a note-taker anyway, so keeping track was no problem. I kept a writing tablet right next to the telephone in the kitchen and used a separate page for each day. Well, at the end of two weeks, I read through my notes, and it was quite a collection! "Can I borrow this?" "Can I drop Jimmy off?" "Can I have a ride to the meeting?" Then I thought about whether I wanted to go along with the requests. You know, as I was reading through some of them, I actually got tense and angry (talk about body signals!). The next step for me was to think about some of those situations, particularly those that I was discontent with and think about how I could have handled them differently had I used the "Assertiveness" steps. For a couple of them, I actually rehearsed out loud what I could or should have said. I was beginning to feel a little more confident in my ability to assert myself.

The first time I tried to assert myself turned out to be a half-success. My cousin Mary Ann called me to see if I could pick up the groceries for the church supper. I started to refuse, but she cornered me and I reluctantly agreed. When I hung up the phone, I realized that I had given in, in-spite of what I had set out to do. I didn't get too upset though, as I had at least *tried* to assert myself. I knew that the next time I would have to be more forceful.

It wasn't long before I had my first successful test of my assertiveness skill. Late Saturday morning, the phone rang. It was Chris—she lives down the street. She wanted to know if she could drop her kids off at our place for a couple of hours. She had an appointment at the beauty parlor, her husband was away, and no one was home to watch them. [1] Well, right away I became aware of being upset, that sort of tightness I get in my stomach when I begin to get tense. [2] This time, I knew what was causing it. "She's got a hell of a nerve," I thought. "I've got things I want to do today and I'm not going to have someone else's kids dumped on me for a beauty-parlor appointment. Let her change her appointment."

[3] So, I quickly thought through some ways I might deal with Chris. I could apologize and make up some excuse. No, I shouldn't have to apologize, I didn't do anything wrong. Or, I could really let her have it! No, that wouldn't help matters any. I'll just tell her I can't take them. [4] "Look, Chris," I said, "I've got some other plans for today, so I can't watch your kids."

"Oh, nuts," she said. "I guess I'll have to figure out something else to do with them."

"Okay, good luck," I said. That was all—no apologies, no giving in. I must admit that I surprised myself and felt a little remorse after hanging up the phone. After all, I could have helped her out. At my expense, though. I really didn't want her kids here. She could find a way without my help. I did have other plans that I didn't want to change. And I did stand up for myself, and the world didn't fall apart. And you know, next time I think it will be a little easier for me to do.

6

Making Changes Stick

If you have accurately identified the skills in which you are weak, carefully prepared yourself and others for your learning or improving these skills, and applied the procedures of Structured Learning, there's an excellent chance you have now learned the skills that were your goal. Yet psychologists and educators have shown repeatedly that a number of things can cause people to forget newly learned skills. They can usually use the skill when they first learn it but, all too often, a week or a month later the skill is gone. Sometimes skills disappear even more quickly, especially when you've rehearsed them successfully with a trusted friend but now have to try them with a stranger, your boss, or an angry spouse. In short, new skills are often fragile and, therefore, no skill training program is complete unless it includes procedures for making changes stick. In this chapter, which concerns transferring skill behavior from where you learned it to where you need it, we will present a number of possible ways you can minimize skill loss. Through the use of these techniques you can both increase the chances of holding on to what you've learned, and sharpen your skills even further.

1. *Be sure your original learning of the skill is sufficient.* Of the several reasons why you may forget a newly learned skill, not learning it well enough in the beginning is the easiest

to correct. You may not have done enough in a couple of areas: Perhaps the way you prepared (setting goals, establishing contracts, getting support) wasn't complete, or you didn't use Structured Learning fully enough. Often, the main reason turns out to be not enough rehearsal or not enough feedback. You can increase the chances that your new skill will hold up over time, therefore, by (a) increasing the quantity of rehearsal before trying a skill in real-life settings and (b) finding better sources of feedback about the quality of your skill use. When you do rehearse a skill, be sure to practice *several* times after you've used it well. Don't stop after only using the skill well once or twice. Keep going, even though you feel you've got it. Psychologists call this "overlearning," and it works!

2. *Be sure your original learning of the skill is realistic enough.* Psychologists have found that the more similar the practice situation is to the situation in which you really have to use the skill, the better you'll retain the skill. That is, sometimes a skill can be learned well but in a form that makes it difficult to transfer the skill to where you need it— on the job, at home, on a date, etc. In a case like this, you should consider such matters as (a) how realistic your original rehearsal of the skill was and (b) how many people and how many different kinds of people you originally rehearsed the skill with. You can make the learning situation more realistic by rehearsing the skill with people and in places most similar to the real-life people and places in which you need the skill. You can make the learning situation more varied by rehearsing the skill with several different people. The greater the variety of other people you practice the skill with, the greater the chances that some of these practice partners will be similar to the people with whom you'll need to use the skill in real life.

3. *Instruct yourself in ways that keep your skill use effective.* As odd as it may seem, psychological research sup-

ports the idea that it is often useful to talk to yourself! This "self-instruction" research shows the benefits of coaching yourself, prompting yourself, guiding yourself, and encouraging yourself. So, to help make your skills stick, we urge you to:

(a) Remind or prompt yourself sufficiently about the skill's behavioral steps when you're in a real-life situation in which you need the skill.

(b) Say encouraging things to yourself—"You can do it!"—rather than dwelling on possible skill failure.

(c) Note the similarities (and/or differences) between a past situation in which a skill worked well and a current situation in which you are less effective in using the skill. If there are similarities, perhaps you should use the skill in a similar manner; if there are differences, you may have to use it (the skill) differently or combine it with other skills, or perhaps not even use it at all and replace it with another skill.

(d) Point out to yourself the specific benefits that will probably accrue to you if you use the skill correctly, as well as the negative outcomes you're likely to avoid in this way.

4. *Maximize the chances that others will reward you if you can use the skill correctly.* When you were first learning a given skill, you may have contracted with other people to have them reward you whenever you used the skill well. But now you've moved to a later stage. You've learned the skill and, although the contract may have helped you do so, the contract is over. You're concerned now with a different question —that of behavioral transfer. Will you continue to use the skill in real life—with people with whom you won't be establishing contracts? How can you increase the chances that *these* people will also reward your skill use? Remember, if others praise, approve, agree, comply, or otherwise reward you, you're likely to keep using a skill. If they complain,

disapprove, disagree, ignore, reject, or otherwise punish you, your skill behaviors are destined to fade away. There are steps you can take to maximize the chances that your correct use of the skill will be rewarded by others:

(a) Say and do things that try to change what others expect of you. Instruct them; change their anticipations about how they expect you to behave; ask them to pay attention to the new things you are doing.

(b) Ask other important people in your life to change their behavior so that it is compatible with or complements or rewards the skill behaviors you're using. Ask your spouse, for example, to use the skills that seem to go along with the skills you are trying to use. For example, ask him or her to respond with "Listening" or "Responding to Your Feelings" when you "Express Affection" or "Express a Complaint." You might even ask your boss to "Negotiate" with you when you are trying to "Negotiate" with him.

(c) Go places, choose times, and select people who are likely to reward your effective skill use.

(d) Avoid places, times, and people that are unlikely to reward effective skill use.

5. *Provide yourself with sufficient and appropriate self-reward for using the skill correctly.* In Chapter 3, as part of writing contracts with yourself, we described rules for when and how you should reward yourself for using your skills well. We introduced these reward rules to help you learn the skills you selected as your goal. You can also use self-rewards to keep what you have learned, and to avoid forgetting skill behaviors. Remember, rewards do not only come from others. You can and should reward yourself, both by what you say to yourself and by things you do for yourself. Self-reward, therefore, is a combination of saying something encouraging to yourself and doing something special for

yourself. You should follow certain rules to be sure that your self-rewards have a maximum effect in helping you retain the skills you've learned.

(a) Choose your rewards carefully. Be sure that the rewarding statement you make to yourself is clear and unambiguous, e.g., "I really handled that well." Be sure that the special thing you do for yourself isn't something you'd do anyhow. For example, don't reward yourself by buying something you already planned to buy. Don't go to a certain movie *as a reward* if you would have seen it even if you hadn't used a skill especially well. A second type of "doing for yourself" reward can be everyday things you got anyway, but that you're now denying yourself until you use the skill well. For example, save that special dessert or expensive cigar as a reward that you can present yourself for good progress.

(b) Always reward yourself *immediately* after you use the skill well, or as soon as possible after. Don't delay in self-reward if it's at all possible. The greater the delay, the greater the chances that your self-reward will fail to serve its purpose of helping to make changes stick.

(c) Be very careful to reward yourself only when you have used the skill well. Saying nice things to yourself *and* doing nice things for yourself should occur *only* when you've followed all the skill's behavioral steps, and done so in at least a moderately effective manner. When your skill use isn't effective, or when you've correctly followed fewer than all of a skill's behavioral steps, we suggest you provide yourself with verbal self-reward only, e.g., "Good try."

6. *Minimize the chances that other skill deficiencies that you have not yet worked on are interfering.* You may have learned a number of the skills described in this book, and chances are that when you set out to use them in real life you (wisely) tried one skill at a time. Getting along effectively in the real world, however, often demands more. Often, a prob-

lem can't be solved or a relationship established unless you skillfully use a combination or a sequence of skills. Before you can learn to skillfully "Express a Complaint," you may have to master both "Using Self-Control" and "Preparing for a Stressful Conversation." Before you can effectively use the skill "Negotiating," you may first have to be equally effective in "Setting Problem Priorities" and "Making a Decision." In general, before entering a real-life situation, it's frequently useful to consider the situation carefully. Ask yourself what skills this situation might demand of you. This type of planning for use of specific skill combinations or skill sequences can often prove quite valuable. There is no magic formula for figuring out which skills you'll need, or in what order you'll need them. Rather, success at planning skill sequences is usually a matter of thinking carefully about what you and the others involved in an actual situation are likely to do. Focus on the actual behavior that is likely to take place. "Let's see," you might say to yourself, "first I'll arrive at the party and I'll have to 'Start a Conversation.' Then I may want to 'Express a Compliment' to the hostess. Harry may be there, and he may try to persuade me to buy season tickets to the football games with him. So I'll have to 'Respond to Persuasion.' Then . . . ''

Work at it a bit and you'll find that even the most complex situations can be broken down into the skills that are likely to be needed. After doing this a while, there is a very good chance you'll become expert at this type of skill-use planning.

We have described six ways you can try to minimize skill loss and maximize the level of skill transfer you are trying to accomplish. If your skill learning still is not as good or as rapid as you wish, you may be applying other aspects of the self-diagnosis, preparation, or Structured Learning procedures incorrectly. To help you spot exactly where the trouble lies, we have included a Troubleshooting Checklist made up of all the ways your effort may go astray. Use it whenever your skill learning is going more slowly than you wish, or when the results you are working toward don't seem to be occurring.

TROUBLESHOOTING CHECKLIST

Complete the following at the first sign of difficulty. Checks in the *NO* column indicate areas that need extra work.

	YES	*NO*
1. Did you select the right skill?	____	____
2. Did you write a behavior-change contract?	____	____
3. Was your behavior-change goal a realistic one?	____	____
4. Were the rewards stated clearly and realistically?	____	____
5. Were the negative consequences stated clearly and realistically?	____	____
6. Did you specify bonus rewards?	____	____
7. Did you keep records of skill use?	____	____
8. Did you get enough initial support from others?	____	____
9. Did you rehearse the skill well enough?	____	____
10. Was the original rehearsal realistic enough?	____	____
11. Did you rehearse the skill with *different* people in *different* situations?	____	____
12. Did you get adequate feedback on how you were doing?	____	____
13. Did you coach yourself (self-verbalize) well enough?	____	____
14. Did you first try the skill with people who were likely to be supportive?	____	____
15. Did the person(s) with whom you tried		

YES   NO

the skill respond in an unreasonable
manner?   ___ ___

16. Did you reward yourself for *progress* with
the new skill use?   ___ ___

17. Did you follow through with your rewards?
Did you *say* and *do* rewarding things for
good skill use?   ___ ___

18. Did you reward yourself soon enough after
using the skill well?   ___ ___

19. Did you follow through with negative consequences for not living up to your contract?   ___ ___

These few words about troubleshooting end our attempt
to teach you how to use Structured Learning for a more
effective and enjoyable life. A reasonable amount of effort
on your part devoted to learning and applying the methods
we have described is very likely to have the payoff you are
seeking. We wish you well and hope you are successful.

7

More Personal Skills

We've done a good bit of research over the past several years to try to identify which skills trouble people the most. The results of this research led us to the skills listed on pages 12–13, which are the same trouble skills that make up the Skill Questionnaire and whose behavioral steps we've provided and detailed in Chapter 5. But those twenty-four skills are certainly not all there is to effective and satisfying behavioral functioning. There are many other skills that make up a good life, and in this chapter we wish to list at least some of them. They may not cause as many people difficulty as those discussed earlier, but they are difficult for some people, some of the time. The preparation, Structured Learning, and behavioral-transfer procedures we described for the most troublesome skills also apply here, and you should use them here as you would for the earlier skills.

SKILL 25: Expressing Appreciation

Steps in expressing appreciation:

[1] Clearly describe to the other person what was done for you that deserves appreciation.

[2] Tell the other person why you appreciate what was done.

[3] If appropriate, ask the other person if there is anything you can do for him or her.

SKILL 26: Expressing Encouragement

Steps in expressing encouragement:

[1] Ask the other person how he or she feels about the way he or she is handling the situation.

[2] Decide if it might be helpful to encourage the other person.

[3] Decide what type of encouragement might be most helpful.

[4] Express encouragement in a sincere and friendly manner.

SKILL 27: Apologizing

Steps in apologizing:

[1] Decide whether there's something you want to apologize for.

[2] Decide how you might best apologize.

[3] State your apology in a warm, sincere manner.

[4] If it is appropriate, offer to make up for what happened.

SKILL 28: Responding to Anger

Steps in responding to anger:

[1] Listen openly to the other person's angry statement.

[2] Show that you understand what the other person is feeling.

[3] Ask the other person to explain anything you don't understand about what was said.

[4] Show that you understand why the other person feels angry.

[5] If it is appropriate, express your thoughts and feelings about the situation.

SKILL 29: Setting a Goal

Steps in setting a goal:

[1] Decide what you would like to accomplish.

[2] Decide what you would need to do to reach this goal.

[3] Decide on the order in which you would do these things.

[4] Judge whether you've planned realistically.

[5] Set a realistic goal.

SKILL 30: Gathering Information

Steps in gathering information:

[1] Decide what specific information you need.

[2] Decide who can give you the most accurate information.

[3] Ask questions, in a direct manner, to get the information.

SKILL 31: Evaluating Your Abilities

Steps in evaluating your abilities:

[1] Decide what ability you need to evaluate.

[2] Think about how you've done in the past when you've tried to use this ability.

[3] Get any outside information you can about your ability (ask others, take tests, check records).

[4] Use all of this evidence and realistically evaluate your ability.

SKILLS 32: Setting Problem Priorities

Steps in setting problem priorities:

[1] List all the problems that are currently pressuring you.
[2] Arrange this list in order, from most to least urgent problems.
[3] Take steps (delegate, postpone, avoid) to temporarily decrease the urgency of all but the most pressing problem.
[4] Concentrate on the most pressing problem.

SKILL 33: Identifying and Labeling Your Emotions

Steps in identifying and labeling your emotions:

[1] Pay attention to those body signals that help you know what you're feeling.
[2] Decide which outside events may have caused you to have these feelings.
[3] Consider all of this information and decide what you are feeling.

SKILL 34: Relaxation

Steps in relaxation:

[1] Pay attention to those body signals that help you know you're tense.
[2] Decide whether you'd like to relax.
[3] Tell yourself to calm down and relax.
[4] Imagine a scene that you find calming and peaceful.
[5] Pay attention to those body signals that help you know you're beginning to relax.

SKILL 35: Helping Others

Steps in helping others:

[1] Observe whether someone needs help.
[2] Decide whether you want to be helpful.
[3] Decide how you can be helpful, and do it.

SKILL 36: Joining In

Steps in joining in:

[1] Decide if you want to join in an activity others are doing (think of advantages and disadvantages, be sure you want to participate and not disrupt what others are doing).
[2] Decide the best way to join in (ask, apply, start a conversation, introduce yourself).
[3] Choose the best time to join in (during a break in the activity; before the activity gets started).
[4] Join in the activity.

SKILL 37: Dealing with Fear

Steps in dealing with fear:

[1] Decide if you're feeling afraid.
[2] Think about what you might be afraid of (think about alternative possibilities and choose the most likely one).
[3] Figure out if the fear is realistic. (Is the feared object really a threat? You may need to check this with another person. You may need more information.)
[4] Take steps to reduce your fear. (Talk with someone. Leave the scene. Gradually approach the fearful situation.)

SKILL 38: Rewarding Yourself

Steps in rewarding yourself:

[1] Decide if you've done something that deserves a reward (something you have succeeded at, some area of progress).
[2] Decide what you could say to reward yourself (praise, approval, encouragement).
[3] Decide what you could do to reward yourself (buy something, go someplace, increase or decrease an activity).
[4] Reward yourself (say and do).

SKILL 39: Dealing with Embarrassment

Steps in dealing with embarrassment:

[1] Decide if you're feeling embarrassed.
[2] Decide what happened to make you feel embarrassed.
[3] Decide on what will help you feel less embarrassed and do it (correct cause, minimize, ignore, distract, use humor, reassure self).

SKILL 40: Dealing with Being Left Out

Steps in dealing with being left out:

[1] Decide if you're being left out (ignored, rejected).
[2] Think about why the other people might be leaving you out of something.
[3] Decide how you could deal with the problem (wait, leave, tell the other people how their behavior affects you, talk with a friend about problem).
[4] Choose the best way and do it.

SKILL 41: Deciding on Something to Do

Steps in deciding on something to do:

[1] Decide whether you're feeling bored or dissatisfied with what you're doing (not concentrating, getting fidgety, disrupting others who are involved in activity).

[2] Think of things you've enjoyed doing.

[3] Decide which one you might be able to do now.

[4] Decide if there are other persons who might like to do it with you, and invite them (propose alternatives, ask tentatively, ask enthusiastically).

[5] Start the activity.

SKILL 42: Dealing with an Accusation

Steps in dealing with an accusation:

[1] Think about what the other person has accused you of (if it is accurate, inaccurate, if it was said in a mean way or in a constructive way).

[2] Think about why the person might have accused you (Have you infringed on his or her rights or property?).

[3] Think about ways to answer the person's accusations (deny, explain your behavior, correct other person's perceptions, assert, apologize, offer to make up for what happened).

[4] Choose the best way and do it.

SKILL 43: Dealing with Group Pressure

Steps in dealing with group pressure:

[1] Think about what the other people want you to do and why

(listen to other people, decide what the real meaning is, try to understand what is being said).

[2] Decide what you want to do (yield, resist, delay, negotiate).

[3] Decide how to tell the other people what you want to do (give reasons, talk to one person only, delay, assert).

[4] Tell the group what you have decided.

Bibliography:
Structured
Learning
Therapy
Research

The reader who is interested in research on the effectiveness of Structured Learning Therapy should see:

Goldstein, A. P. *Structured Learning therapy: Toward a psychotherapy for the poor.* New York: Academic Press, 1973.

Goldstein, A. P., & Kanfer, F. (Eds.). *Maximizing treatment gains: Transfer enhancement in psychotherapy.* New York: Academic Press, 1978.

Goldstein, A. P., Martens, J., Van Belle, H., Schaff, W., Wiersma, H., Hubben, J., & Goodhart, A. The use of modeling to increase independent behavior. *Behavior Research and Therapy,* 1973, *11,* 31–42.

Goldstein, A. P., Sherman, M., Sprafkin, R. P., Gershaw, N. J., & Glick, B. Training aggressive adolescents in prosocial behavior. *Journal of Youth and Adolescence,* 1978, *7,* 73–92.

Goldstein, A. P., & Sorcher, M. *Changing supervisor behavior.* New York: Pergamon Press, 1973.

Goldstein, A. P., Sprafkin, R. P., & Gershaw, N. J. *Skill training for community living: Applying structured learning therapy.* New York: Pergamon Press, 1976.

Sprafkin, R. P., Gershaw, N. J., & Goldstein, A. P. Teaching interpersonal skills to psychiatric outpatients. *Journal of Rehabilitation,* 1978, *44,* 26–29.

Index

A

Accusation, dealing with, 129
Action, deciding on, 129
Affection, expressing, 16
Affection, 71–72
  skill use, 71–72
  steps, 71
Anger, expressing of, 17–18, 77–79
  skill use, 78–79
  steps, 77
Anger, responding to, 124–25
Apologizing, 124
Appreciation, expression of, 123–24
Assertion, 25
Assertiveness, 107–9
  skill use, 108–9
  steps, 107

B

Behavior changes, permanence of, 113–20
  checklist, 119–20

original learning, 113–14
overlearning, 114
realism of learning, 114
reward likeliness, 115–16
self-instruction, 114–15
self-reward, 116–17
skill, decay of, 113
skill deficiencies, 117–19
Behavior description, 47–48
  and steps' identity with skill, 47
Behavior feedback, 51–52
  from other person, 51–52
  realism of simulation, 52
  self-examination, 51
Behavior rehearsal, 48–50
  in imagination, 48–49
  openly and alone, 49
  openly with other, 49–50
  openly with target person, 50
Behavior transfer, 53
Being left out, dealing with, 128

C

Complaints, dealing with, 21–22
Complaints, expressing of, 16–17, 72–74

skill use, 73–74
steps, 72–73
Complaints, responding to, 90–92
  skill use, 91–92
  steps, 90
Compliments, expressing of, 15,
    65–66
  skill use, 65–66
  steps, 65
Compliments, responding to, 18,
    79–80
  skill use, 79–80
  steps, 79
Contracts with self for behavior
    change, 34–39
  and behavior-change goal, 35
  and bonuses, 37
  example, 38–39
  and negative consequences, 36
  record-keeping, 37–38
  and rewards, 34, 35–36
Contradictions, dealing with, 21
Contradictions, responding to,
    88–90
  skill use, 89–90
  steps, 88
Conversation, ending of, 14, 61–
    63
  skill use, 62–63
  steps, 61
Conversation, preparing for a
    stressful, 23, 93–95
  skill use, 94–95
  steps, 93–94
Conversation, starting of, 14, 59–
    61
  skill use, 60–61
  steps, 59

D

Decisions, making of, 23, 95–96
  skill use, 96
  steps, 95

E

Embarrassment, dealing with, 128
Empathy, 80–82
  skill use, 81–82
  steps, 80
Encouragement, expression of,
    124

F

Failure, response to, 20, 86–88
  skill use, 87–88
  steps, 86
Fear, dealing with, 127
Feelings, responding to, 18–19

G

Goal-setting, 125
Group pressure, dealing with,
    129–30

H

Help, asking for, 15–16, 66–69
  skill use, 68–69
  steps, 66

Help, from others, 39–42
 and contracts with others, 41–
  42
 discussion, 39–41
 as reinforcement, 39
 support and responsiveness, 41
Help, to others, 127

I

Identification, of emotions, 126
Information-gathering, 125
Instructions, following of, 19, 82–
  84
 skill use, 83–84
 steps, 82
Instructions, giving of, 16, 69–70
 skill use, 70
 steps, 69

J

Joining in, 127

L

Listening, 15, 63–64
 skill use, 64
 steps, 63

N

Negotiations, 24–25, 100–07
 rehearsal, 105–6

skill use, 101–7
steps, 100

P

Persuasion of others, 17, 74–77
 skill use, 75–77
 steps, 74
Persuasion, responding to, 19–20,
  84–86
 skill use, 85–86
 steps, 84
Problem, naming of, 11
 pinpointing, 11
Problem priorities, setting of, 126

R

Relaxation, 126
Responsibility, determining of,
  23–24, 96–98
 skill use, 97–98
 steps, 96–97

S

Self-assessment, 6
Self-control, 24, 98–100
 skill use, 98–100
 steps, 98
Self-evaluation, 125
Self-reward, 128
Skills:
 in action, 57–59
 choice of first target, 33–34

deficiency in, 5
difficulty, scoring of, 29
incompetence of advice on, 5
learning, 8
list of, 12–13
and steps in, 57
strengths versus problems, 27
Structured learning, 6–7, 45–47
and action change, 46

activeness of, 46–47
and attitude change, 45

T

Tasks, concentration on, 22, 92–93
skill use, 92–93
steps, 92

BEHAVIOR-CHANGE CONTRACT

Behavior-Change Goal: _____

_____

Behavioral Steps to be Followed:

     1. _____

     2. _____

     3. _____

     4. _____

     5. _____

     6. _____

     7. _____

Reward: _____

_____

Negative Consequences: _____

_____

Bonus: _____

_____

Record-Keeping: _____

Beginning Date: _____ Ending Date: _____

    Signature: _____

BEHAVIOR-CHANGE CONTRACT

Behavior-Change Goal: _____

_____

Behavioral Steps to be Followed:

     1. _____

     2. _____

     3. _____

     4. _____

     5. _____

     6. _____

     7. _____

Reward: _____

_____

Negative Consequences: _____

_____

Bonus: _____

_____

Record-Keeping: _____

Beginning Date: _____ Ending Date: _____

    Signature: _____

BEHAVIOR-CHANGE CONTRACT

Behavior-Change Goal: _____

_____

Behavioral Steps to be Followed:

     1. _____

     2. _____

     3. _____

     4. _____

     5. _____

     6. _____

     7. _____

Reward: _____

_____

Negative Consequences: _____

_____

Bonus: _____

_____

Record-Keeping: _____

Beginning Date: _____ Ending Date: _____

    Signature: _____

BEHAVIOR-CHANGE CONTRACT

Behavior-Change Goal: _____

_____

Behavioral Steps to be Followed:

     1. _____

     2. _____

     3. _____

     4. _____

     5. _____

     6. _____

     7. _____

Reward: _____

_____

Negative Consequences: _____

_____

Bonus: _____

_____

Record-Keeping: _____

Beginning Date: _____ Ending Date: _____

    Signature: _____

BEHAVIOR-CHANGE CONTRACT

Behavior-Change Goal: _____

_____

Behavioral Steps to be Followed:

      1. _____

      2. _____

      3. _____

      4. _____

      5. _____

      6. _____

      7. _____

Reward: _____

_____

Negative Consequences: _____

_____

Bonus: _____

_____

Record-Keeping: _____

Beginning Date: _____ Ending Date: _____

    Signature: _____